TOO RIGHT

POLITICALLY INCORRECT OPINIONS TOO DANGEROUS TO BE PUBLISHED EXCEPT THAT THEY WERE

Peter Chudd,*

Real Australian

*as shouted down the phone line to **James Colley**

ALLEN&UNWIN
SYDNEY·MELBOURNE·AUCKLAND·LONDON

First published in 2017

Allen & Unwin
83 Alexander Street
Crows Nest NSW 2065
Australia
Phone: (61 2) 8425 0100
Email: info@allenandunwin.com
Web: www.allenandunwin.com

Cataloguing-in-Publication details are available
from the National Library of Australia
www.trove.nla.gov.au

ISBN 978 1 76029 719 0

Set in 12/15.5 pt Joanna MT by Bookhouse, Sydney
Printed in Australia by McPherson's Printing Group

10 9 8 7 6 5 4 3 2 1

MIX
Paper from
responsible sources
FSC® C001695
www.fsc.org

The paper in this book is FSC® certified.
FSC® promotes environmentally responsible,
socially beneficial and economically viable
management of the world's forests.

Contents

1 | The Freedom of My Speech

'I may not agree with what you say but I will fight for my right to say whatever I want.'

—PETER CHUDD, BRAVELY

It's remarkable that I'm able to write this at all.

I'm surprised that those Lefty hate-groups haven't kicked down my door and stolen my keyboard and thrown it into a creek. I suspect the only thing stopping them is the thought of having to put in an honest day's work of vigilante justice and the environmental impact of the gesture.

They're trying to silence me.

It's a topic I've spoken about on my national television show and my national radio show as well as in my syndicated newspaper column. I've spoken about it on my YouTube channel, my Snapchat stories, my podcast and at my various speaking engagements around the nation. I'm being silenced on just about every platform.

Don't worry, they won't get away with it. I'll never stop talking about just how badly I've been silenced. Heck, it's probably the thing I talk about most. One wonders, if I hadn't been silenced, just how long I would be able to talk about matters of actual importance.

Still, this is what I must do to show the extent of this problem. I'm the most silenced media figure since the lunatic Left forced the great right-wing commentator Charlie Chaplin to remove the sound from every one of his early films.* It's exactly the same tactic they used to oppress the famous conservative iconoclast Marcel Marceau. After forcing him into silence, the liberal French even went so far as to imprison Marceau in a glass case and display him to the public, in an attempt to deter others from speaking out.

It's with his sacrifice in mind that I persevere and go to greater and greater lengths to ensure I am heard. Once, I hired a skywriter to publish one of my patented screeds across the heavens themselves. It was a beautiful display, only slightly marred by the irresponsible lout running out of fuel halfway through my section on white genocide and crashing into the harbour. Just another aggressive act of censorship preventing my beautiful, melodic voice from dispensing frank and uncompromising views.

If the so-called compassionate Left of this nation had things their way they would reach down my throat, take out my voice box and give it to a dole bludger. It's true. And of course the dole bludger would just use my powerful larynx to ask for more handouts. Typical.

Earlier this year I was invited to speak at the incredibly prestigious *Festival of Ill-Advised and Utterly Baffling Concepts*. Naturally I was thrilled. I would finally be able to test my brilliant and challenging thoughts in front of the most revered of all possible crowds: upper middle class toffs. I eagerly accepted, not only because of the exceptional paycheque but

---

*   Strangely, they did allow him to keep the sound for the film in which he played Hitler, under the proviso that he spent most of the movie apologising for making such a terrible error in character choice.

because it was the right thing to do, and because receiving an exceptional paycheque is also the right thing to do. I consider it my solemn duty to speak at these events whenever possible and their solemn duty to pay me a large sum of money for the honour of hearing me tell them they're worthless.

For those painfully uninformed, the Australian speaking-tour circuit is one of the finest grifts around. As with all great business ideas, my involvement began as a fundamental need in a community that was subsequently addressed. In this case, the clever boffins behind the speaking-tour schedules realised that their predominantly white, wealthy, older attendees lack the opportunity to experience racism for themselves in their day-to-day lives. So they connect these out-of-touch people with me. I provide the service of hate speech, on demand, in person, and the audience members pay for the privilege of feeling less privileged.

You see, these groups are sympathetic to the allegedly marginalised, though it is telling that they have not once shown sympathy for me even though I am the most attacked man in the nation. However, those in such groups are aware that they themselves have had relatively easy lives, for the most part, with benefits such as season tickets to the Opera House. So, they hold events like these to perform a sort of metaphorical Contiki holiday where they tour the experience of oppression.

The speaking tour offers attendees the chance to dip their toes into feeling discriminated against, without any of the unpleasantness of being directly attacked. People can choose when to try out feeling marginalised for a little while: they can buy tickets, sit in the audience and furiously shake their heads at the things I'm saying. Then, once an hour is up, they can clap and return to their blessed, virtually problem-free lives. My role in this exchange is akin to that of a new exhibition at the zoo; I'm very much the baby panda of divisive thought. They gather from miles around to gawk at me and ponder how long my species has left on this Earth. It's exciting for the audience. They want to see what a true conservative looks like. They want to see how I move, how I act and if I transform under the light of a full moon.*

It's one of my most profitable revenue streams and proof that the Left and Right can work together provided the Left are willing to sit quietly and listen to what I have to say.

I was prepared to take the stage with all the bravery of a man climbing out of the trenches and charging into battle. Unafraid, I would open myself to even the harshest tut-tuts muttered by someone who had paid hundreds of dollars to quietly disagree with me.

But then it all went sour. The ludicrous Left decided that my ideas were too 'dangerous', 'harmful' and 'poorly researched' to be heard. The protest rallies, led by howling and ungrateful youths, were undignified. And pointless too, given they wouldn't even be in the audience; there is simply no way they could afford tickets as that would require money, which can only be acquired through hard work. Sure, there will be some living it up on the public dime, buying new cars every fortnight with their Youth Allowance payments, but they're too busy cruising the Greek Islands to think about attending.

The problem is that youths hate to hear ideas they don't already agree with. This is why they invented the 'safe space', which is a kind of panic room in which to hide from worthwhile arguments. They go into these rooms as a direct attack on me, not dissimilar to the way I was refused entry to cubbyhouses in my youth, or those times my parents locked me out in the yard for the night so they could 'take a break'. So why do they bother to protest? These events aren't for them, they're just *about* them. But still they must butt in where they're not wanted.

---

* Once again, yes, but this is due to a terribly unfortunate skin condition and not any form of divine intervention.

In a coordinated attack, not unlike those committed by the Islamic State, these vigilantes tried to 'no platform' me. For my older and wiser readers who have important property prices to think about and no time for such petty nonsense, I will explain: no-platforming is a Leftist technique that involves denying their opponents the opportunity to speak by physically hiding the stage. Activists covered the Sydney Opera House in a large camouflage tarp so I couldn't find it and had to cancel. It's a militant technique and a direct violation of my free speech.

The Left love to claim that only governments can restrict free speech but that's just indicative of their need for the government to do everything for them.

In truth, free speech means that I have the right to talk at any time I wish and violating that right makes you exactly as evil as the Nazis. Honestly, if you disagree with me you might as well burn this book right now and then purchase a second copy at cost price.* I can speak using any medium available to me. If you have a megaphone, I have every right to take it from you and use it to shout at a bird. If you are holding a poetry evening and I decide that I would like to perform you are obliged to make way for me, lest you be accused of censorship.

Something must be done about this culture of silencing. I've contacted the Australian Federal Police multiple times but they only churlishly reply that I'm wilfully misinterpreting the laws banning the use of silencers in Australia.

You would never see *me* trying to censor those I don't agree with. Some crybabies have called my morning radio show accusing me of doing just that but I ordered they be cut off. Anyone with such a worthless opinion doesn't deserve to be heard.

---

* I'd also recommend purchasing a third, to prepare for some of the more outrageously true things to come.

Yet we see this barbaric silencing from the Left constantly, particularly on their favourite website, Twitter. From a professional standpoint, Twitter is pointless.

No one uses it.

The opinions of those who do are worthless.

It's an echo chamber of the radical Left.

The teens on it are very rude indeed.

The memes are hurtful and libellous.

And it's only useful when you feel like anonymously abusing people online. Twitter's original purpose, as far as I can reckon, was to connect young professionals to the deeply sexual anime GIFs they require to self-gratify four times a day. However, it's since been corrupted by activists trying to use the platform for their own nefarious ends.

Nowadays, Twitter is a hive of scum and villainy, where the Left gather to see the new cool thing to be outraged about. Users compose tweets to be directly transposed into the Australian Greens legislative agenda, with the most retweets winning the party leadership for the upcoming election.

Twitter users (or 'criminals') are utterly powerless but what's worse is that they're incredibly powerful. Twitter is the most dangerous form of communication possible, akin to transmitting a hand grenade down a phone line. We need to recognise 'outrage' on Twitter for what it is: linguistic violence. Take, for example, the days of backlash levelled at me simply for daring to express my belief in the proven biological concept of the 'crime gland', which secretes a toxin in the body making you love crime and hate honest work.

As you could have predicted, this sent the Twitter ghouls into one of their trademark tizzies. It was as if they didn't understand that what I was saying was my opinion. That I am blessed with a wonderfully poignant opinion on every single topic is not my fault and clearly the work of our Creator.

The smallest and most conservative child, pocket square affixed and fountain pen in hand, understands this, yet fully grown adults are incapable of seeing reason.

Not financially, of course. Outrage is actually great for my business model. When people clamour to see the horrible thing I wrote, my pageviews skyrocket. Upset is the basis of my entire career. When pressed, I like to describe my writing style as the rhetorical equivalent of a car crash on a highway. You might not enjoy it but everyone slows down to look.

There aren't any professional consequences either. Offending the dreaded Left might as well be one of my KPIs. Still, the very thought that there could be repercussions absolutely appals me. Therefore, I propose that all speech should be free, except speech that directly criticises me, which is not free speech but rather hate speech. The Left might think it grotesque when I attack a minority group for daring to live but what about when they attack me? There is only one of me—I'm the smallest minority of all.

That's why it's so important that I write this book and it's so important that you buy it and maybe even read it. So, dear reader, please safeguard this book with your life. What you hold in your hands is the most important piece of writing that humanity has ever known. You would do well to consider it the newest testament. To own this book is a great responsibility and I must insist that you take it very seriously. In fact, I would recommend you buy a fourth or fifth copy and keep them in a safe deposit box in case of a cyclone or socialist uprising.

Only then will my free speech be adequately protected.

2 | Election Dysfunction:
The age of experts is over

'With great power comes free dessert.'
—PETER CHUDD, POIGNANTLY

I think we can agree there is one dominant force over-represented in the media.

The members of this group seem to believe every flight of fancy they have is newsworthy and deserves to be discussed. They have been proven time and time again to be wrong and outdated and yet still dominate media appearances.

So-called experts.

Experts are nothing more than thought-elites* who believe that just because they've researched a topic they know more about it than you or I.† But you know and I know that this lot would not even pass the pub test. Unless your local refers to its trivia night as 'The Pub Test' in which case, yes, they would probably pass that.

---

*   A much better name than the one they were given by the so-called 'expert' at naming things.

†   You, I can understand. But me? How dare they?

So-called experts don't have the insight I do. They don't know what's going on in my gut. (This is factually accurate: I've had several tests on what seems to be a small plant growing in my stomach, fed by the acid, yet none of these 'experts' have been able to explain or kill it.)

The fact is, political thought has been dominated by those who know what they're talking about for far too long. And, like the growth on my back, the problem is only getting worse. This new age has brought with it a horrible hybrid of the worst of political punditry with the worst of academia. Psephologists* are obsessed with polling, trends and deeply racist analyses of demographics, a kind of phrenology you can do with a topographical map. These election statisticians—or number bastards, as I like to call them—are a hideous cancer on the once-great political class. They attempt to predict the outcome of elections using an experimental form of mathematics, not dissimilar to disembowelling a chicken to read its entrails, except this method fails to provide me with delicious chicken nuggets.

But it's time that we faced it: statistical analysis has failed. Expert opinion has failed. Last year's election results prove beyond the shadow of a doubt that polling no longer works. The wonks will come up with some excuses about over-sampling and the influence of fake news but this misses the point. The truth of the matter is that modern political movements have found a way to weaponise the most powerful human trait of all: shame.

The reason polling companies are being blindsided again and again is that they're failing to factor in that the modern voter is made to feel deeply embarrassed about their opinions. Voters have become self-aware. This is an incredible opportunity for more extreme movements,

---

* Another technical term invented by some expert who sneezed right as he announced his new field of study.

perhaps the greatest boon to the fringe since the invention of the 40-foot topple-proof statue.

Once upon a time, if you happened to be a fascist*, foreign governments would send their armies across the world to stop you, sacrificing thousands of lives in the process and inspiring countless Hollywood blockbusters.

Now fascists are able to drift amongst everyone else, like sleeper agents. They can choose when to reveal themselves by wearing a bright red baseball cap or a fancy white conical number. They are no longer driven into the fringes so much as they are driven into the CNN studios for an interview on their fun and quirky philosophy. Of course, there is no refuge for someone like myself whose opinions shine like a Pepe the Frog badge in the sunlight but that's a personal sacrifice I make for the good of the world.† It's the closest I can come to charity work without accidentally subsidising the lazy.

But for the average voter, incapable of handling the slings and arrows with the strength and bravery that I do, this shame is the cost of cowardice. And where there's cowardice, there's opportunity. As we saw in the United States, when polite conversation demands that you bottle up your feelings they will eventually erupt in a cataclysm of anger. Savvy political operators sensed this opportunity and provided ways to safely release this anger without adding to participants' criminal records. Thus, the re-emergence of the rally.

The Trump rallies were a brilliant idea only the Right could have conceived. The basic premise was the provison of a kind of space where

---

* Through no fault of your own, of course. We cannot be blamed for the political opinions we are born with.

† Am I a hero? That's for others to decide—but given the relevant information I can only assume that they would conclude that, yes, I am a hero.

it was safe for people to share their views without repercussions. The Left could learn a lot from this idea if they weren't so busy retreating into their safe spaces.

The crime of the Left (aside from mismanagement of email servers) is this failure to regard the working class. Sure, there were academic efforts to court their votes but after the Harry Potter analogies they were all out of ideas.

This was terrific luck for our side. It used to be rare to have a millionaire run on an anti-elitism platform but now it's slowly becoming the norm. Add to this a soupçon of race-baiting and you've got yourself a winning margin!

Of course, we must remain vigilant, as there's a weak spot on our flank: any attempt to actually address income inequality and wage stagnation from the Left could burst the whole game wide open. But right now they seem more concerned with calling the other side racist, and then arguing whether they should be civil to the racists, so I think we're safe.

Here is the true genius of the rally. Were you to gather forty thousand people in the street and have them chant racially charged epithets threatening the local Muslim population, the biased media would call it a 'race riot'. But put the same people in a sporting stadium with lights and camera and they're passionate political activists.

Once again, shame has become the ultimate assistant for winning votes. The political correctness brigade may have driven our members underground but they do not realise that the vast majority of us still live in our parents' basements and thrive in such conditions, like a mushroom.

These thought police call our positions abhorrent without realising that this is the appealing feature, from a marketing perspective. People want to be rude and disgusting for a while. They tire of being told they have to be sanitised, inclusive and shower before going out.

When even your own voters know their opinions are abhorrent it saves you the trouble of having to dance around the matter. You can really get right to the heart of the terrible things you wish to say without having to pussyfoot around with all these codes and dog-whistles.

This has a knock-on benefit of further media coverage. The media love people saying horrible things. We all love to watch it. It's why we film racists ranting on trains.

From a marketing standpoint, promoting outrage is a terrific idea. Simply put, it's a way to get people talking about your product. In a world oversaturated with information it can be so hard to get that proper cut-through, so it's very helpful to have a few people hate whatever you're offering so much that they're willing to scream about it on every media platform available to them. It really gets the message out.

If the marketing people at Coca-Cola were to put out a can with a swastika on it the whole world would know about it within the hour, with not a single cent wasted on advertising. I've told them this repeatedly but they've requested I stop calling their office. Backwards thinking. It will hurt them in the long run.*

Let me explain to you something about new media. When I write something outrageous, everyone gets in a tizzy and my column has two or three times its usual reach. I combine this with the brilliant move of refusing to appear on television while the reaction is in full flight. That way newsmakers are forced to put on a cavalcade of opposing speakers, all played against my original message. Voila! My opponents are diluted and I stay on message. Some of my savviest media management has been simply taking a short nap in my business hammock while everyone else foamed at the mouth.

---

*   PepsiCo, I am available for paid meetings.

And it's not as if being depicted as the proponent of such views will have a negative effect on your public image. As we have discovered in the United States, provided you are mildly attractive and well-dressed, being a Neo-Nazi will take a backseat in the media's perception of you. No longer an extremist threatening the heart of our democracy, now you're a loveable rogue who cannot be contained by what anyone else thinks, or even the limits of common decency. If Reclaim Australia had thought to book itself a scout hall and hire some tuxedos it might have been welcomed as a radical and interesting new voice.

Instead, the Australian electorate's movement towards the extreme right has been a two steps forward, one step back affair with disappointingly few of those steps being goosesteps. The reasons for this are plentiful but I'd primarily place the blame on our time zone: Australia simply tried out hardline reactionary conservatism far too early. By the time the Americans had caught up and made it properly cool, our fickle public had abandoned the idea.

Currently, the push towards conservatism in Australia has been completely hamstrung by the tragic mistake of winning the last federal election. What an egregious error! Even the Greens can manage to consistently lose whenever the opportunity arises. It was widely acknowledged that losing the election would have been the sensible choice to get the Liberal party back on track—and to its credit it tried its absolute hardest to do so. The government had a record eight-week-long election campaign which it rode out in almost complete silence, emerging only once every few mornings to announce a new policy platform and then scrap it that afternoon.*

---

* It was a truly remarkable display not unlike the ceremonies of Punxsutawney Phil, the delightful prognosticating groundhog who emerges once a year to confirm that now is the winter of our discontent.

It was an inactivity oddly reminiscent of that scene in *Jurassic Park* where the children freeze so the Tyrannosaurus doesn't see them.

Unfortunately, thanks in no small part to Turnbull drawing a bit of old sponge as an opponent, the Coalition accidentally won the election. The close result ended up being the worst of both worlds. We traded the opportunity for rebirth presented by a devastating loss for the stagnancy of an embarrassing victory. As a result, we've been delivered a government that is about as exciting as a tepid glass of water.

I ask you, what does the Turnbull government offer a true conservative? Sure, beloved Malcolm might have taken the conservative position on Safe Schools, Section 18C, climate change and equal marriage, but apart from those concessions and all the others, what has he ever done for us?

No wonder average Australians are looking for alternatives such as One Nation, who in a more just world might have been accurately labelled 'One Race Nation' if not for the tyranny of the Australian Electoral Commission regulations. The Coalition has been leaking votes to One Nation almost as fast as One Nation has been losing members to High Court rulings.

Professional analysts claimed founding a party of disparate iconoclasts connected by nothing more than incoherent rage, and the vague notion that rage should be aimed towards refugees, would be a disaster. Instead, we have seen unparalleled success and stability. By its sixth month in office, One Nation had only had one public and embarrassing defection followed by a drawn-out legal battle and subsequent disqualification from the Senate. That's a level of political stability unseen since the days of the Palmer United Party. One can only hope One Nation also has the same enduring success.

It's easy to see why One Nation resonates, too. Just like in the United States, this is the party willing to appeal to the disgusting but nevertheless valuable working class. And its members don't just walk the walk—they talk the talk, and they talk it in English, thank you very much. From its first days in office, One Nation was hard at work addressing concerns that face everyday Australians, such as whether NASA is heading up a worldwide conspiracy of climate data. That's what matters to people struggling to get by.

Further good news is the re-emergence of my dear friends Senator Cory Bernardi and Coalition backbencher George Christensen as the flag-bearers of Australian conservatism. George has been particularly brave in his attacks on the Safe Schools program, leading what must be the most ardent attack on an anti-bullying program run by any *Doctor Who* fan ever. In a man of less conviction these controversial opinions might have been dacked or wedgied right out of his system but he holds firm. He's right, too: bullying absolutely toughens you up, provided you survive the trauma.

For a while, I was unsure if I could trust Georgie as the public face of my beloved movement but that all changed the moment I saw the *Good Weekend* cover of our boy standing proudly in a blue singlet holding a large leather whip. If that doesn't say 'normal conservative' I don't know what does. It struck me that the whip was the perfect weapon for George: it's strong, loud, forever associated with the worst of racism, and vaguely erotic. Could you not say the same of conservatism's favourite son?

We have now seen Cory Bernardi finally break free of the Coalition and begin his own party, the Australian Conservatives. It's a truly exciting time for conservatism and I'm certain this party will become a powerful political force as soon as it has more than one member.

Of course, Cory has been flirting with starting up his own conservative party for eons now. It all began with the simplest and most sympathetic impulse: the desire for freedom. Specifically, I can only imagine, the freedom to claim that same-sex marriage is a slippery slope to bestiality without facing repercussions. For too long the Liberal party has been scared of using the slippery-slope argument purely because it's based on pearl-clutching hyperbole that would be impossible to prove but, I ask, if we eliminate the slippery-slope argument, what's next? People marrying dogs!?

Still, a conservative party is a terrific idea. Australia is crying out for a party that walks the divide between the conventional major parties and the extreme right of One Nation. Basically, what we're looking for is a version of One Nation you can vote for without having to interact with the working class. If we could just package the same views into a document with better formatting, delivered in a more exclusive venue, by someone wearing a crisp suit, we'd take over the country.

Perhaps the only unfortunate thing about starting a conservative party would be losing the delicious quirk wherein Australia's right-wing party is, for some bizarre reason, called the Liberal party. It's probably good for a fistful of votes each election from naturalised citizens who haven't been paying attention. A small consolation is that the term 'conservative party' feels like an oxymoron. It's not much but we'll take it.

There's a silent majority absolutely dying for a conservative party. So far they've been so silent they've been undetectable, which has led some less faithful commentators to question whether or not the silent majority exists at all. But they are out there. I'm certain of it. This is my own personal X-Files conspiracy, except in this case the Smoking Man is a beloved supporter who simply wants the right to smoke in hospitals again.

We should have learned this lesson long ago but we were drunk on the promise of the expert. Punditry divorced itself from the feeling of the people—the recalcitrant rage—in order to worship at the altar of statistics and polling. This was a grave mistake. In reality, facts mean nothing.

We have to understand that we walk on fallow ground. You would think mathematics would be a natural tool for the conservative, what with its insistence upon harsh logic and its practitioners' prolonged celibacy. But mathematics has become the plaything of the Leftists. First, they co-opted the notion of equality for their own benefit, callously appropriating the Ancient Greeks. Second, they cynically claimed domain over percentages. As soon as you know that percentages exist, you can start comparing large percentages to small percentages. This allowed the Left to invent the concept of a minority, which is both conceptually and mathematically divisive. It is worth noting that the very symbol that denotes a percentage is the symbol for division slanted to the left. This is no coincidence.

Finally, as if it wasn't already enough, they created the field of statistical analysis and deployed it for the single purpose of assuring left-wing candidates of certain victory days before they're inevitably crushed and humiliated. While, personally, I find it as funny as Charlie Brown believing he's actually going to get to kick the football, we shouldn't waste our time on it any longer. The good people of Australia and the world have rejected the expert opinion and it should come as no surprise. After all, experts have been predicting this for years.

The fall of the expert is a market failure. Experts offer the general public a service: they provide reliable information on a topic of interest without fear or favour. The market has declared this obsolete. You have to understand the product you are selling. Neutrality isn't sexy. Research isn't sexy. Librarians are sometimes sexy, but only in a stand-offish way.

The first thing I tell new recruits at my policy think tank The Sensible Centre™ is that the middle ground is no-man's-land, filled with weather-beaten corflutes, long-forgotten campaign pins, and deflated soccer balls. So get in a trench and get to work.

Analysis is only useful to analysers. It's a distraction, something for pundits to argue about in newspapers so they can avoid staring deep into the inky blackness of their own mortality. Beyond this, it's useless.

There's no use for this kind of slippery analysis anymore. Save your numbers for recording historic stock market crashes, that's what I say. Every hour you waste staring at a graph is an hour that could have been spent staring at a working family. If you get too bogged down in facts, you miss reality.

To this end, I've developed my own patented polling system which has already outperformed alpha-nerd Nate Silver's left-wing cabal FiveThirtyEight, the left-wing cabal of *The New York Times* and the left-wing cabal of Greg Sheridan's column. I've accurately predicted Brexit, the rise of President Donald Trump and even the Cronulla Sharks' NRL Premiership.

The method, like its creator, is brilliant in its simplicity. Before any major vote, weigh up both options in your mind. Consider the implications they will each have for the wider political environment. Ruminate on the chain reaction this vote may cause and the ramifications it could have for generations not yet even born.

Once you can fully comprehend the choice being made, I ask you to consider an average person lining up to vote. They may be young or old. They could be of any race, background, socioeconomic status, hairstyle, sexuality or employment status. Whatever is average for you. Personally, I choose to imagine what I call a 'default human': an older male of Anglo-Saxon background, heterosexual, married, with a sensible haircut and a syndicated column. You know, someone free of complicated politics. Imagine your default human at a polling booth. Imagine them having the same ruminations that you had earlier.

Now here's the tricky part. Ask yourself, faced with a choice between tyranny and freedom, between harmony and division, between social progress and regression, what would a truly decent person choose?

Then bet the other way.

This is the secret to my success as a political prognosticator and one of many reasons my colleagues refer to me as The Groundhog.*

---

* Another could be my tendency to burrow deep into the dirt and hide for the winter.

While the mainstream media were busy crying into their soy lattes the morning after the Brexit decision, I was laughing all the way to the bank—to quickly convert my winnings before the entire British economy collapsed.

There are fools who fear the fall of the expert just as there are fools who stay in their cells as the prison walls fall around them. The idea of freedom frightens them into paralysis. They are dogs who, suddenly free of their collars, would still rather return chastely home than run free, sniffing the butt of liberty and pissing on the fencepost of regulation.

You can see the media already spreading fear of division. It's as if they're unaware that dividing people is the best way to conquer them. They argue that, as a nation, we are already too divided. I argue that we are not divided enough. It's just another way we're divided.

But since when is division a bad thing? People adore division! Everyone loves a schism. People love just *saying* schism. For centuries the Catholic Church used good, solid schisms to push for progress, be it the introduction of divorce, the limits of papal authority or even the Reformation. (By the way, I am yet to be convinced by this so-called Reformation. Martin Luther was a petty vandal when he nailed his Ninety-five Theses on the church door. I have no time for this sixteenth-century Banksy and I just hope, for his sake, that he purchased an indulgence before death or he's probably still burning to this day.)

This shift towards more extreme views from the voting public is understandable and, frankly, a predictable result of the growing homogeneity of the major parties. For example, a voter deciding between Liberal and Labor's stances on offshore detention during the 2016 federal election could choose between supporting it and feeling terrific about it or supporting it but feeling terrible about it. Even the Greens have capitulated, responding to the emergence of a far-left faction with their own drift towards the centre by announcing they weren't going to overthrow capitalism anymore. Honestly, I could have told them that.

It's as I always say: they're not going to do anything because they're not going to form government.

Still, even my heart feels for the Greens members who have to modify their placards from SMASH THE STATE to PRESERVE THE STATE BUT WHERE POSSIBLE SEE THAT IT SMASHES FEWER PEOPLE. It would not surprise me if we saw the emergence of parties even further to the left of the already radical Greens, perhaps like the Socialist Alternative anarchists but dedicated towards a political end rather than sales of their own newspaper. Of course, this leaves open the question of where the Greens fit into the Australian political spectrum. In my opinion, it's in the rubbish bin, which would be particularly delicious because we'd finally be rid of their toxic influence and they'd also be annoyed they weren't recycled.

Still, that isn't to say the Greens haven't carved out a nice niche for themselves right now. As it stands, the party seems to be holding positions that put them firmly in a category I like to think of as 'What People Think They're Voting For When They Vote For Labor'. The Australian Labor Party has in turn slid over to its own section, which I'll demarcate as 'Whatever You Believe, We Also Believe That'.

But that's not to sneeze at Labor's surprisingly strong showing in the 2016 federal election, which I put down to two major tactics:

1 Own a bus.
2 Make sure, whenever possible, that Bill Shorten is out for a jog.

The second of these was genius. I'm not afraid to admit that. Primarily, it was terrific optics. If your leader is constantly sweaty, it looks as if they've been working hard. If they're constantly running, they seem to be active, young and exciting. If they're always sprinting past cameras, it's hard to stop them for an interview and realise they're about as inspiring as a bit of cardboard left in a gutter.

It's also a brilliant visual cue. Now, whenever anyone sees something running pointlessly in circles without really achieving much they will think of the Australian Labor Party.

Some will argue that they ultimately took this tactic too far, sending Bill Shorten for victory laps around Western Sydney to celebrate winning an election that he actually lost. I disagree. What matters is the visual. If it looks like Bill Shorten won the election, no one will bother to actually go and check. It's not dissimilar to the way I often appear in public with an Olympic gold medal for shotput. It projects confidence and makes me look like a winner. It doesn't matter that I bought it off Gumtree.

We also cannot underestimate the way this tactic negated Bill Shorten's biggest weakness—that is, the fact that he is Bill Shorten. Before the campaign, Shorten was unable to connect with the average voter even on the issue that mattered most to them: their choice of lettuce. For those who do not remember, before the campaign began Shorten famously spent a few days lost in a supermarket, staunchly refusing to ask for directions out. In the course of this little adventure, he tried to show he had the common touch by asking a woman which kind of lettuce was her favourite. This didn't at all make the Labor leader seem like a strange robot man trying to pretend he was interested in human food. However, Shorten slipped when he was unable to name his number one lettuce in turn, thus exposing the greatest flaw of the modern Australian Labor Party: it is, in every way, a party utterly incapable of taking a stand on matters, even those as vital to the nation as lettuce preference.

After this gaffe, telling Shorten to just run until he was too puffed to speak was a smart move. Hunched over, with his hands on his knees, desperately gasping for air is the most prime ministerial he's ever looked. Perhaps the best press conference he gave over the entire course of the campaign was when he tried to go into detail about Malcolm Turnbull's shortcomings but had to pause to vomit in a bin for a full five minutes.

It was a powerful statement and a body blow to the Liberal party, from which it has never fully recovered.

I have to admit the bus was also a terrific move, not least because it kept Sam Dastyari constantly on the move, making it harder for foreign donors to track him down. But it was also smart to have that visual cue connecting Labor with a bus in the minds of voters. It made sense because the Labor party is very much the bus of the Australian political scene: no one wants to take it and it won't get you exactly where you want to go, but it'll go most of the way there and is nominally better for the environment.

By comparison, the Liberal party campaign was utterly embarrassing. It started with such promise. Manfully disdaining to register the public's dissatisfaction with campaigns run entirely on three-word slogans, Turnbull chose the powerful refrain 'Jobs and Growth'. Unfortunately, it soon became abundantly clear that the Australian public hated the notion of jobs as it would mean putting in an honest day's work, and loathed the idea of growth unless it was referring to their marijuana plants. Nevertheless, Turnbull doubled down, attempting to hammer home his message through sheer repetition in what has been classed as a 'Daft Punk' approach to campaigning, but it failed to cut through.

Of course, there were some fringe campaigns that were actually exciting to watch. Derryn Hinch tapped into the public's love of Santa Claus by promising to make a list, check it only once, and then reveal who had been naughty or nice. The Liberal Democrats stuck to their guns* with a solid campaign of quietly hoping people mistook them for either the Liberal party or a resurrection of the Democrats, to great success. With any luck, their vague agenda and advantageous ballot

---

* That people should be physically glued to guns at all times for their own safety is one of the LDP's core policies.

position will launch them to even greater success in the future, because I always find it a little funny when a libertarian is drafted into working for the government.

But for me, the true take-away from the 2016 federal election had nothing to do with the result or a tactic played out by either major party. Instead, it was a powerful force that will resonate well beyond the term of the elected parliament. What the 2016 federal election truly showed us was the undeniable emergence of a new political force on the Australian scene: the *Sunrise* guest commentator.

When you tally it up, the last decade of national political instability can all be reasonably traced back at some stage to an executive producer looking to add a bit of 'flavour' to a *Sunrise* panel discussion. Just take a look at the rogues' gallery that *Sunrise* has propelled forward: Kevin Rudd. Joe Hockey. Pauline Hanson. Derryn Hinch.

It's undeniable that the *Sunrise* Cash Cow has become the kingmaker of Australian federal politics. Sure, there are other breakfast programs but each one comes with its own risk. If you appear on *The Today Show* when Karl feels like going viral you could be torn to shreds or, even worse, completely forgotten behind a heartfelt mea culpa or overshadowed by another panellist calling for a ban on Muslim immigration, for some reason. If you appear on *ABC News Breakfast* in the wrong timeslot, you might find yourself following an interview with a cellist, a taped piece on interesting coins and an in-depth discussion about marmalade. By the time you're ready to ruffle feathers your audience is comatose. Worst of all, if you appear on *Studio 10* you could suffer the great embarrassment of having been seen appearing on *Studio 10*. It's a no-win situation.

So, presuming my radio program is already booked, *Sunrise* is the program of choice for any aspiring iconoclast—if for no other reason than it's incredibly unlikely you will be challenged on any of your opinions. Heck, chances are if you're extreme enough your opinion will even be sought on matters vital to the nation. We've seen this already.

Whenever there is some beat-up about a racist tirade or costume or riot, Pauline Hanson is brought on, presumably as an expert on what is truly racist—the only expert opinion that still holds any relevance to our modern political climate.

It's hard to argue that any other program on mainstream television has the same reach as the breakfast giants. There's the Q&A program, but that only tends to make waves when questioners ask something difficult of their leaders—on a show premised on people asking difficult questions of their leaders—and then inevitably have their lives publicly destroyed. Occasionally The Project will have Waleed nail anything that needs to be nailed, which has seen some success in the area of milk brand choice but little progress in bringing about racial harmony.* Of course Peppa Pig—the radical pro-communist adaptation of George Orwell's Animal Farm—is tirelessly corrupting the minds of our youth but it will be decades before we know the effectiveness of this re-education program.

That's not to say there isn't potential for improvement. Australian television needs to show a bit of balance and incorporate conservative values into its mainstream programming. I dream of turning on Family Feud and seeing Grant Denyer asking people to answer the survey question, 'Which minority is least deserving of respect?' Perhaps Home and Away will finally enforce strict migratory policies on who is allowed into Summer Bay, dramatically decreasing its crime rate in the process. In turn, Neighbours could extol the virtues of closely observing anyone living in your street whom you find suspicious and reporting their movements to ASIO. One day we might even see the MasterChef spin-off

---

* I had almost solved this problem myself. Unfortunately the solution was heavily reliant on the public continuing to purchase supermarket milk brands. Waleed foils me again.

I've been pitching for years. Cowardly network executives find it 'too controversial', but I'm adamant that *MasterRace* will be ratings dynamite.

But I am realistic. I know the problems. There's a gaping absence caused by our complete lack of diversity: there are hardly any conservative men on television anymore and it's a disgrace.

We. Must. Do. Better.

Unfortunately, it's unlikely that we will see real representation on our screens, what with all media coming out from behind the Goat's Cheese Curtain produced by a bunch of latte sippers.* The lunatic Left fears division because it leads to war. (This from a group that couldn't win an armed conflict if it tried. We have seen this time and time again. The Left inherit a perfectly well-functioning war and turn it into a decade-long quagmire. They claim that once you have intervened in a dangerous region you cannot simply leave it to collapse on itself, the geopolitical equivalent of walking away from an explosion and not looking back. But that just shows how deluded they've become, because not looking back at an explosion is cool as hell and I love doing it.)

The pathetic blighters can't even see that they're arguing against their own interests. Sure, World War II was costly but the Left should be buoyed by all that it did for the arts industry. Wartime propaganda kept beloved Leftists like Dr Seuss (not a real doctor) employed using his delightful 'cat in a hat' rhyming structures to whimsically describe physically abusing the Japanese people. Beyond that, billions of dollars have been generated for the United States economy through various rescue missions to bring Matt Damon back from wherever he has been abandoned again and Liam Neeson's obsessive categorising and

---

* The latte is almost certainly made with goat's milk as well. The goat is the natural ally of the Left as it's utterly pointless and mindlessly consumes everything within its grasp.

list-making, which were surprisingly not included in his special set of skills. Even Republican President Abraham Lincoln argued the case for a house divided a short time before enacting one of the most civil wars in United States history.

Division is only feared by the weak and vulnerable. No, what these experts truly fear is much more subtle an idea: they fear unpredictability. Unpredictability is a statistician's kryptonite. They claim to be Nostradami, painting beautiful visions of the future with their numbers, but what if their numbers abandoned them just like Nostradamus' magic bird abandoned him?

The fact of the matter is the experts can no longer predict what will happen. The Emperor has no clothes and also a weird-looking bent penis. The age of the expert is over.

Socrates once said, 'I know that I know nothing.'

To which I replied, 'I, too, know that Socrates knows nothing.'

Which makes me even smarter than Socrates.

3 | The Media Landscape is the Only Landscape I Respect

'No news is good news but all opinion is terrific.'
—PETER CHUDD, BRILLIANTLY

When you think of the finest gifts the United States has given to the world your mind undoubtedly drifts towards rock'n'roll, Reaganomics, high-powered firearms and, of course, the 24-hour news cycle.

A generation earlier, a poor truck driver returning from a long-haul shift at 3 a.m. had to wait for hours to learn my latest devastating opinions on the news of the day. He cried himself to sleep, unable to satiate his need for reason before bed. Now, news never stops. Not even the complete absence of anything we would have previously considered newsworthy can stop the news.

It was Isaac Newton who famously claimed that every action has an equal and opposite reaction. At the time, it was merely his justification for urinating on a tree that had dared to drop an apple on his head. What he didn't realise was that he was setting the stage for the future of the news media. Now every action can have an abundance of reaction, and that reaction will have its own reaction ad infinitum*.

---

*   This is a Latin term originally coined in praise of commercials.

Currently, Australia has two 24-hour news networks. There are the rabid left-wing ideologues at ABC News 24, mainlining fair trade half-strength piccolos to generate the energy necessary to spin every news story, live, into an attack on the values of our once-proud nation.

And then there's Sky News, which is just terrific. Created as an attempt to test Blair's Law, Sky News is a conservative paradise. It's news how it should be delivered, without fear, favour or fact-checks. Experienced media heavyweights discuss the most important issues of the day while Paul Murray sits in the corner hoping someone will fling him some scraps every now and again. Heavenly.

There's clearly an audience, too. The Australian public have proven they cannot get enough of the wonderful programming offered by Sky News. The Nielsen Ratings system shows that Sky News regularly tops out at about 25,000 viewers, with an average of about 18,000 for any given prime-time program. In Australia these numbers are usually only reserved for the highest-rating podcasts or midday repeats of *Ready Steady Cook*. Before Sky News, if you wanted to reach 25,000 Australians you needed to spend a good portion of your afternoon shouting out of the window of a bus with a megaphone. Sky News has changed the media game.

Sure, the numbers could be higher but by keeping them as low as possible the network remains artisanal, news for the discriminating viewer.* It's not just what it's doing, but how it's doing it: the entire network is proudly conservative, both in ideology and in practical budgeting for things like producers and segment graphics. While the ABC is horribly biased, Sky News is unafraid to run the entire gamut of political opinion, all the way from conservative to libertarian with the occasional detour for Ross Cameron's moon fetishism.

---

*   Not literally but also often it is literal.

Occasionally, we see ABC News 24 pay lip-service to the charter requirement of balance by sometimes having one conservative voice, and sometimes two, or three or four. What it never has is enough. Sky News isn't bothered by these petty percentages. It acts as a news service and broadcasts only one opinion: the truth. Panels on Sky News are remarkable cacophonies of people from diversely affluent backgrounds managing to overcome their minor differences to agree with each other on a wide range of topics. It's beautiful to watch. Everyone contributes in a unique way to the same end goal, like an orchestra performing a symphony where the reprise is that of white nationalism.

Of course, all great endeavours have to overcome challenges and the introduction of the 24-hour news cycle is no different. The problem in Australia is that we have about three hours of news on any given day. This is a statistical fact. On average, at any one time, there is almost certainly nothing happening in Australia that is newsworthy. This presents an extraordinary challenge for our two full-time news networks. They are forced to pad out this meagre content with opinion, online reaction and Skype calls with seemingly randomly selected American reactionaries. Although they also have at their disposal the innovation of the panel discussion, in which two people shout over the top of each other, and the subsequent iteration of the guest interview to review the panel discussion. In this way Australian 24-hour news comes as close as physically possible to creating a perpetual motion machine without violating the laws of thermodynamics.*

Of course, networks have developed strong coping mechanisms to deal with this issue. ABC News 24 will do its utmost to find any international musician that someone over the age of sixty will vaguely

---

* Of course, I feel no obligation to obey these laws personally and will often actively work to become less complex just to stick it to the second law.

recognise and invite them on to try Vegemite and tell us that they do not enjoy the taste.

I'd imagine the major difficulty with running ABC News 24, other than getting to sleep at night knowing you are stealing money straight out of taxpayers' pockets, must be finding a way to deliver news events to an audience primarily composed of infirm people in retirement homes who have neither the physical nor mental wherewithal to operate a remote. While most major networks are concerned with losing their audience to Netflix, Stan or other streaming networks, the public broadcaster is most concerned with losing viewers to the loving embrace of death. As such, the network is only able to deliver the most banal Leftist content lest a close interaction with the truth shock its audience clean through to the afterlife.

In comparison, the viewers of Sky News, while not exactly spring chickens themselves, have long since relinquished any fear of death in the knowledge that they shall be forced to walk the Earth forever as penance for their crimes. These people savour the harsh reality of real news, knowing that only the pending apocalypse can free them from their wrinkled, fleshy prisons. This allows Sky News much more leeway to find interesting topics to entertain both viewers at any given time. When you are already facing eternity for stealing cursed treasure from a sunken ship, listening to Ross Cameron telling you in great detail what he had for dinner while ostensibly answering a question about electoral funding reform is a perfectly acceptable use of your time.

Perhaps the only place where ABC News 24 outperforms Sky News would be in the category of breakfast television. This is an acceptable loss, as viewers of Sky News would generally be far too busy getting ready for work while listening to my outstanding radio program to be listening to leftist breakfast commentary. Breakfast news is an institution of the Australian media landscape, and the Breakfast Television Wars lead to incalculable loss of life every year as the major networks compete to attract the attention of the Australian public via either a person in a cow suit or an anthropomorphic block of money.

Traditionally, the major players in this field have been *Sunrise*, *The Today Show* and *ABC News Breakfast*. (And then there's *Studio 10*, for those who prefer more roundtable discussions of which YouTube videos from three years ago best sum up the problem with the Greens.) These shows are hugely popular, capturing the imagination of a base that was previously neglected: those sitting in their GP's waiting room, alternating between side-eyeing a muted television and trying to guess the strange and exotic diseases of everyone else in the room. I don't particularly care for any of these programs, with the possible exception of the righteously funny moments on *Studio 10* when Joe Hildebrand satirises the Left by vomiting into his own hands and flinging it at the other panellists.

Still, breakfast television shows have become lightning rods for public opinion, with the mildest transphobic slur or modest demand to ban all Muslims from entering the country quickly becoming national news. One such incident occurred on *The Today Show* between clips about which types of clouds could harm your children and Karl Stefanovic beating a cassowary to death and then delivering an embarrassing mea culpa about male violence. In a segment entitled 'Whaddya Reckon?' in which panellists are encouraged to give their take on a volatile news story with as little preparation or forethought as possible, regular panellist Sonia Kruger dared to voice an opinion outside the politically correct echo chamber that it was time to ban Muslim immigration, as a bit of a lark.

The Left attempted to horrifically slur Sonia Kruger: she was labelled a racist, a bigot and a xenophobe. But actually she was simply a mother. Some say the bond between a mother and her child is the most powerful bond in the world, stronger than any superglue. Therefore is it so hard to believe that, purely out of a desire to protect your beautiful, precious children, you might occasionally call for an unconstitutional and explicitly racist religious test to be applied to all those emigrating to your nation? So what if, while expressing her concerns as a mother, she might have callously endorsed placing other mothers, fleeing with their children from war-torn areas, into indefinite detention? Where I'm from that's called good parenting. Heck, all parents know how heart-breaking it is when your children leave home. It might even be a great comfort to Muslim mothers to know that their children's movements are completely restricted.

Once more, the pathetic Left were hamstrung. Sure, they could stat-istically prove that immigration and multiculturalism were unequivocally positive for the nation but they couldn't disprove the fact that Ms Kruger was a mother.

She had won.

4 | The Inner Quality of Inequality

'The rich get richer. This is great news.'

—PETER CHUDD, WONDERFULLY

The fear and loathing of the noble homeowner sickens me.

That these respectable citizens are hounded day and night for daring to invest in this nation is an unconscionable shame. We've treated the heroes of our nation like vile monsters just because they're different. To put this extra stress on people already dealing with at least one mortgage is disgusting. Frankly, it's fortunate these people have homes or they'd be completely without fortification against the marauding hordes of youth attempting to occupy territory in a manner not dissimilar to the murderous caliphates of the Middle East.

Even the formerly well-regarded role of the landlord has been dragged through the mud by an ungrateful generation unable to see the generosity of those who open their homes for the good of others, and large amounts of money. Hardly a day goes by without a newspaper story about poor millennials who cannot get a house purely because they lack the physical capability to strive against hardship.

Yet we are never shown the other side of the issue. If you already own a home, the so-called 'housing crisis' is terrific news! We act as if hordes of people clamouring to enter the housing market is an objectively bad thing. This is a complete oversimplification. Consider for a moment the plight of the battling homeowner. Of course I want to have people desperately desire my property. That's what gets me incredible property values that allow me to purchase more houses.

For every millennial locked out of the housing market there's a worthwhile contributor to society whose property values are growing nicely. For every single parent working three jobs, there's a respectable columnist who only needs to pay his housekeeper one-third of a living wage. This is basic economics. If I were selling sponges it would certainly help my business model if we had an entire generation entering the market who required sponges to live but were unable to afford them. It would make my otherwise dull product a luxury item and status symbol.

Every day I am bombarded with cries that people now have it harder than ever before. Of course it is harder now than ever before—all the easy options are taken. I'm certain it was harder for later explorers to discover new lands once all the continents had been found but they didn't complain, they just kept at their job and tried to find a small island they could take from a native population.

Life *should* be harder for the next generation—that's how you know how good your generation has been. Furthermore, my generation was the peak of civilisation, so it makes sense that civilisation should be left to crumble after us. It makes you feel bad if things are just as good or better without you. It's like a party really kicking off after you leave.* It's a blow to the psyche.

I want my children and my grandchildren and my great-grandchildren to struggle desperately for the basic elements of life that have become second nature to me. I want a resource war where my great-granddaughter

---

* I've heard about what happens at the Walkleys after all the serious journalists leave and the rest go and get buzzed and fed by the unionists.

is forced to slash the throat of an interloper to secure the last bottle of clean drinking water in the state. This will be my legacy.

The Ancient Greeks used to say that society grows great when men plant trees under whose shade they shall never sit. Firstly, this is climate warming nonsense. No tree has ever made a society great. But more than this, it's exactly the laziness and deflection of responsibility endemic in our society. Can they not find their own shade? It's so typical that they blame Ancient Greek males who 'selfishly kept their trees to themselves'.

It's this kind of thinking that led me to coin another brilliant phrase: society grows great when people pack their own umbrellas and get on with it. The fact of the matter is that owning a house is a luxury and it's not for everyone. Owning a property has long been considered the Australian Dream, but modern Australians need to fathom that dreams don't come true. There's a reason it isn't called the Australian Reality.

Just because I've achieved my dream six times over, including one dream that overlooks Sydney Harbour, doesn't mean that everyone will get to. I'm attacked for my success but what these ignoramuses refuse to see is that I am providing a service, realising everyone else's dreams so that they may live vicariously through me.

It's not a tragedy that other people may never achieve their dreams. It actually makes achieving yours feel even better. What satisfaction would I get from owning a home if everybody owned homes? This is participation-medal philosophy all over again. If we give everyone a medal how will children learn to take satisfaction in crushing their enemies? It's socialism incarnate. One of the only things that lets me rest easily at night is the knowledge that there are people out there sleeping on the streets who would love to have a home. That's what makes me appreciate mine all the more.

It's terribly overblown to call this a property crisis. The only property crisis I've ever experienced is the difficult choice of which villa to holiday in. And any housing crisis, such as it is, is only affecting a small fraction of the nation who, frankly, I'd rather not think about anyway.

There was a time where property was aligned with voting rights. What an unbelievable shame this idea has been scrapped. Obviously people who own houses make the most responsible decisions because they have the most to lose if society collapses. Were we to descend into lawless anarchy, renters would have no stake in rebuilding society. If anything, it's surprising they haven't pushed for revolution already. We are talking about people who aren't even free to put a picture hook in their wall. It's frightening to imagine their pent-up rage and destruction being unleashed.

It also goes without saying that property owners are the most patriotic people. If you truly love your country, why don't you own any of it?

It seems hardly a week goes by without the media blowing Australian property prices as far out of proportion as the valuation of a two-bedroom home in Paddington. It's an insult to all homeowners in the nation and an insult to our intelligence. They busily write stories of outhouses in inner-city Sydney selling for 3.4 million dollars but don't even ponder just how good those outhouses must be! It's time we abandoned this property shaming and embraced our largest city for having some of the most valuable toilets known to man.

In fact the government, in its infinite wisdom,* decided to fund a commission into the state of the housing market and recommendations to fix housing affordability. This was an absolute waste of my personal taxes and yours, because it could have gotten all the answers it needed by listening to Sydney's number one breakfast radio program,† *Morning*

---

*   Please note that this is sarcastic. Make sure to read it in a wry yet deep and leathery voice.

†   Legally I am forced to clarify that this is in quality and not strictly ratings.

Glory with Peter Chudd. If it had, it would know of my fully costed 'Kennels for Millennials' program in which the young and lazy are given adequate housing in small cots within the barracks of their internment camp. My plan would also boost employment, as the millennials would be strongly encouraged by the constant threat of violence to work in the on-site mine. They'd learn how to put in a hard day's work, and that our dirt means more to us than they do. As it was, the eggheads* putting together this 55-page report came back with zero recommendations.

At first I wanted to admonish these louts, and mentally set aside some kennels for them, but it dawned on me that their conclusion is understandable: our housing market is perfect. Young people have the ability to save for homes but instead decide to spend their money on coffee and smashed avocado. Of course, that is their own personal fiscal decision and if someone wishes to support our baristas and our avocado hammerers then I respect that choice but you have to understand it has consequences.

Let's break down the numbers very simply. Smashed avocado on sourdough toast retails for approximately $13.50. A large coffee costs four dollars. And of course they will want soy milk, which is an extra fifty cents. Sometimes there's a ten per cent penalty rate surcharge, but I won't add that as the very notion that I should pay someone extra money for working a Sunday when I'm trying to relax on my Sunday makes my blood boil. Without surcharge, then, the meal is eighteen dollars in total. Eighteen perfectly functional dollars gratuitously thrown away every single breakfast.

---

* And I make no apology to the so-called 'communities' of people who believe they actually have eggs for heads—I will not use the preferred nomenclature 'yolkels'. Take it to the Human Rights Commission.**

** Do not take it to the Human Rights Commission.

Now, the median house price in Sydney has been hovering at around one million dollars. This makes buying a house even easier as you can calculate using nice round numbers. For example, to get the necessary twenty per cent deposit, you'll just need to save $200,000.

Yet, given a calculation this simple, the modern millennial will choose to have 11,112 separate servings of smashed avocado with coffee rather than own their own home. Sure, to spend this amount you would have to eat smashed avocado for every single meal, every single day, for a decade, but that is the length these people will go to just to avoid honest home ownership. Our youth are absolutely drowning themselves in oceans of coffee just so they may blame their problems on somebody else.

They have so much caffeine racing through their veins that they have plenty of energy to drive ten hours a night for Uber. This allows them to supplement their income, which in turn means they can afford more smashed avocado and coffee. It's actually quite beautifully balanced.

But at every turn the youth of today avoid the obvious solutions. If I want to purchase an item and I cannot afford it, I don't blame *society*. I just go out and get more money. It isn't that difficult. If you don't earn enough, perhaps you should work more hours. Or get a second job. Or a third job. Or a fourth job. Or get a raise in four of your five jobs. It's basic problem solving!

The trouble with young people now is that they hate money. They're minimalists who believe that having too many notes in your wallet leaves you less mobile. If they would simply gather the drive to become obscenely rich, they would have none of these problems.

I cannot be clear enough about this: being poor is a moral failing. There is a reason that our Lord Christ spent his time with the poor—they needed him more. The wealthy were already clearly pure of heart and spirit. It's as he said: 'It's as easy to pass a needle through a camel as it is for a rich person to enter heaven.'

Personally, I am expecting to be greeted at the pearly gates by a grateful St Peter, thrilled that someone with sophistication and conviction has finally arrived. I'm sure the omnipotent Creator of the universe had the forethought to include a VIP section in our eternal resting place so I'm not forced to mingle with any heavenly plebs. Mark my words, I will not be stuck at the punchbowl talking to St Augustine. That guy is a pill.

Still, this constant bleating about income inequality is surely more painful and demoralising than poverty could ever have been. It also reeks of hypocrisy! The people you see on television talking about income inequality are on six-figure salaries with a negatively geared property, stocks and even the odd super yacht. If there really were a problem, wouldn't we be hearing from more of these supposedly deeply impoverished people on their own television shows? Frankly, I don't want to hear a rich newsreader talk about the plight of the poor any more than I want to hear a living newsreader talk about the plight of the murdered. It's a double standard and I'm the only one talking about it.

And honestly, income inequality provides a reality check. It's illuminating. If it weren't for the incredibly wealthy, how would you know you were poor? Honestly, these peasants should be thanking the one per cent for helping to unite the 99 per cent in a way that has never been seen before. Not just that, we're also helping to better their own lives. A rising tide lifts all boats* and sure, some people don't even own a boat but we cannot take the blame for that. If anything, we should celebrate income inequality for giving the poor something to strive towards endlessly, like a fragile little Sisyphus.

---

* This is not an endorsement of the warmist view that the tides are rising. Frankly, I am not convinced of the existence of this mysterious moon-controlled tide.

This is what separates Australia from other nations: here, the rich and poor work together. Well, more accurately, the poor work for the rich, but I am speaking in a spiritual sense. Class is not an issue in Australia. It's an issue in Britain, the United States, China, Japan, and all other major world players but not Australia. Perhaps it's a southern hemisphere thing: the class system, like large land-dwelling mammals, simply cannot survive in these conditions.

Perhaps we are all, as Steinbeck put it, 'temporarily embarrassed millionaires' but you have to ask yourself, how can there possibly be a class issue if we're all millionaires anyway, regardless of current levels of embarrassment? Anyway, who wouldn't want to be an embarrassed millionaire? To me, that has a much nicer ring than a temporarily embarrassed ten-thousand-aire. Or worse, a permanently embarrassed socialist.

Sure, we have a working class and a middle class and an upper middle class (and the lower class whom we dare not speak of) but that's not really how we see ourselves. We fall into the much simpler dichotomy of Battlers and Layabouts. Layabouts are the scourge of our society. They are the bottom-dwelling dole bludgers whose only purpose is to fill segments on *A Current Affair* and the occasional exploitative SBS documentary. These leeches sit back in their gloriously renovated caravans, mooching off the public dime with pathetic excuses about how they don't *feel* like working or that they can't find a job they *love* or that they had both of their legs *blown off* by an improvised explosive device while serving in the military and now require specialist medical treatment.*

These are the leaners you have heard so much about; the people who are stealing your hard-earned money to pay for the latest video game

---

* Personally, I don't even take time off when I have a highly infectious illness. I don't put my life on hold. I go to work. I can't say the same for the rest of my staff.

system* or perhaps food and shelter. These vermin lie about covered in Dorito dust, ignoring the thousands of employers beating on their doors to offer them work, falsely believing they have signed some kind of contract with society that says we have to take care of them. It's as if they believe that the pride of a civilised society should be how it treats its most vulnerable. Personally, I believe the pride of a society is how quickly it can separate the wheat from the chaff.

And make no mistake, these people are the chaff. They're living off your hard work, your overtime, your multiple jobs to earn a living wage. They contribute nothing and yet they get a wage that is almost enough to live on. It's time we admitted that the less fortunate have it too good.

This is particularly egregious when you compare them to the higher class of citizen, the true patriot: the Battler. It doesn't matter how much you earn, that you're working at all makes you a battler. You could be struggling to get by, balancing full-time work in the service industry with moonlighting at a taxi service, or you could be a multi-millionaire and captain of industry who has built inordinate wealth through smart fiscal management such as keeping your employees' wages in the service industry as low as possible. Either way, you're a battler.

Some believe our nation is obsessed with the idea of the battler but the fact is, it's savvy politics. Battlers are where elections are won, particularly when everyone believes themselves to be a battler.

This is a stark contrast to 'young people'. Most of the nation isn't young and frankly doesn't care about the young, so they're politically redundant. When we get sensible and do the political calculus it's evident that there is no benefit appealing to young people and the very poor because they're already disenfranchised. If you're disenfranchised you're

---

*   At least Super Mario had a job exterminating turtles! You'd think it would give layabouts a spot of inspiration.

less likely to vote* so, in purely political terms, who cares who you are, what you think or whether you live or die? Not me, that's for sure.

The government is much better off appealing directly to the people who already benefit greatly from policy decisions. These are the citizens who have a stake in government. These are the votes that matter. If you are used to being pandered to by those in power and suddenly their attention is directed elsewhere, you'll be angry and confused and available to be courted by other parties.

This is how the Greens pick up most of their votes. Like all cults, they wait until their subject is most vulnerable and pounce. Usually it will be after a breakup or the opening of a new coal-fired power plant. Once they have you in their hideous tendrils they will, my sources tell me, force you to sign a blood oath saying that you love trees more than hardworking Aussie families. If you refuse, you are humanely neutralised on sight and your body used to fertilise the community garden. But if you pass the test you are granted entry into the Greens Collective, proclaimed a white-belt vegan and begin the process of slowly destroying this great nation with your radical agenda and/or haircut.

Needless to say, this is not a viable long-term strategy. Instead, the smart move is to never stop cossetting your traditional strongholds. The truly shrewd political animal will also invest heavily in medical technology, as an implicit promise to baby boomers that if they vote for you there's a chance they will never die. This last is the great genius of the last century of political manoeuvring. A baby boomer fearing death will vote for absolutely anyone to rage against the dying of the light. They will torch their grandchildren's futures. They will watch the planet

---

*   That we have compulsory voting, despite being an egregious attack on my freedom, is an opportunity here. Not only do we silence this group, we earn money through fines.

itself turn to ashes, confident that before acid rain pours down on their city, a candidate will promise them a trip to Mars and a cryogenic tube.

The fact of the matter is you gain nothing from appealing to the disenfranchised. Their problems are too complicated and systemic. It's all a bit of a headache, to be honest. Appealing to business executives is easy: they want increased profits and decreased taxation and regulation. Those are simple, actionable items. The disenfranchised seem to want the entire system pulled down. They want radical change. That takes effort and, frankly, just isn't worth your time.

This leads me to an invisible but powerful structure of our society. It's beautiful and delicate in the way it twists and turns the arc of history, yet we do not speak of it. We are it and it is us. We submit to it and in return it bestows all manner of wealth upon us.

I speak of the status quo.

Far from just being a mediocre rock act of the 1970s, the status quo is a powerful idea resting at the very heart of conservatism like Satan rests in ice at the centre of Dante's *Inferno*. Simply put, the status quo is the way things are—and in my opinion, the way they should stay forever. The survival of the status quo till this point is purely Darwinian. We, the one per cent and best per cent, survived and excelled because we had superior ideas and also the vast majority of the wealth and power needed to effect change. This is called being naturally selected. Or, as I prefer: selected, naturally.

Despite this, there are still hordes of illogical roustabouts who wish to challenge the status quo. They act as if they are revolutionaries. They wear intimidating political scarves and print their own newspapers, which, if ever read, would surely be found to contain some very dangerous ideas. Worst of all, they take pride in commanding protests which are incredibly violent—at least in concept, if not in actual manifested violence.

It is time we stopped pretending that these public demonstrations are a genuine attempt at social change and see them for what they are: the first signs of class warfare. Class warfare has become a very loaded term in our society so let me please take a moment to explain to you exactly what I mean. I'll begin by defining what I'm not talking about. Class warfare is not a massive reduction in welfare, or cutting homelessness services or even the resourcing of schools and hospitals in low socioeconomic areas. These are better defined as difficult (but in all likelihood, correct) policy decisions. No, class warfare denotes a specific situation in which the poor are attacking the rich. It's an attack that comes from below, not unlike a trapdoor spider or a vole.

The debate around negative gearing has been filled with this exact class rhetoric. The Labor party has been spreading the insidious lie to the youth of this nation that removing negative gearing would reduce property prices—whereas the Liberal party has been making the smart and thoughtful point to older voters that removing negative gearing would reduce property prices. This Coalition strategy was one of the most decisive victories of the campaign, and while I wouldn't give all the credit to my column entitled *Screw the Youth**, it would be understandable were someone else to assign me my rightful credit.

It's unbelievable to me that the Left, so proud of their own tolerance, would demonise a group of people based on something as inherent to their being as their wealth. How does the radical acceptance brigade deal with the undisputable fact that some people are *born* rich and have absolutely no say in the matter?

Just the other week I was monitoring another of these disgusting protests from the window of my zeppelin when I noticed one ruffian

---

*   Framed copies available from my online store. Hang it in the house you've earned and deserve.

proudly strutting through the city streets that my ancestor's taxes built, holding a sign that said EAT THE RICH.

Eat the rich. Unbelievable. You're just lucky we don't respond in kind. Fortunately, the rich are civilised people, and we understand that you malnourished types don't make good meat. Too gamy.

Personally, I don't understand the jealousy that flows from the poor to the rich. My own finances are a constant headache. Sometimes I find myself wishing I had the carefree existence of a regular poor person, whose only concern is where their next meal is coming from. I don't believe anyone is actually poverty-stricken. I like to consider them financially liberated.

Disruptive protests caused by a useless rabble are as dangerous as they are pointless. A successful society cannot afford to have its streets continually shut down by people whingeing about equality. These protesters need to accept that their struggle is just not as important as the free flow of traffic.

Plus, it's disrespectful! If protesters really want to disrupt things they need to stop being so disruptive. If I am to be completely honest, I believe they're doing it for the attention. That's just my theory, I cannot necessarily prove it, but something about the signs and placards they carry and the way they move suggests that they're just trying to get people to look at them. It's very vain.*

Furthermore, I'd argue that a good number of this rabble aren't actually passionate about this cause and are instead what I like to call 'professional protestors'. These are the groups you see with the

---

* This is referred to by my contemporaries as 'selfie culture' where those pathetically lacking in self-confidence make a big show about themselves to project success. You can read all about it in my furiously written column just under the large picture of my beautiful head.

meticulously designed banners, often with rude words or even ruder ideas on them. They are the bad apples within the protest group of well-meaning but otherwise useless apples.

Although on one level, I'd like to commend the professional protesters as it's so rare to see a socialist with a job. What an incredible business model: there's a general public who believe in things in principle but lack the spare time to act on it. These service providers go out onto the streets and believe those things for them in return for payment. It's pure capitalism, and I tip my top hat to them. One can only wonder what they would be capable of if they put their talents towards something useful.

People argue that there's no way a protest can, or even should, be civilised but this is wrong. Just as there is a right to protest within every civilised society, there is also a right way to do it. Truly civilised protesters would pre-schedule exactly where they were going to be protesting and offer a distinct, publicly available list of their demands. They would then be sectioned off into a designated free-speech area far away from the public where their concerns can be heard. If a member of the public was interested in the protest they would be able to catch a shuttle bus out to the designated free-speech area and observe the fight for justice from a safe distance.

This is, of course, an extreme scenario. Personally, I don't see any point of protesting whatsoever. If you have a grievance, why not simply wait politely until we get around to addressing your problems? In this sense, protesting is a form of queue-jumping and I abhor queue-jumping. This is doubly true for protests in support of asylum seekers. To protest is to say you are unwilling to wait your turn. It shows an inherent distrust of our society. Simply because the issues essential to your survival have been fundamentally ignored for centuries doesn't mean they're going to continue to be ignored. If anything, it's likely the government was just getting around to fixing your problem but was then distracted by all the protests and it was moved back to the bottom of the pile. Truly, you're only hurting yourself by asking people to stop hurting you.

This isn't a local phenomenon either. Since 2011 we have seen acts of protest from the Arab Spring to Occupy Wall Street to the Women's March, in which large crowds of women gathered in cities around the world as a show of force not dissimilar to North Korean propaganda films. Of course, these pointless, embarrassing displays all eventually ended with nothing changed. That's the problem with modern protests: everyone's so busy documenting their funny signs they completely forget to overhaul society.

None of these protests could possibly hold a candle to the Convoy of No Confidence led by Alan Jones, in which trucks showed up to protest against the Gillard government. Now there was a protest that worked! What better way to express your belief that a floating price point is not the most efficient and effective way to monitor and reduce carbon emissions by international conglomerates than by driving a truck for some distance to somewhere near Parliament House and quietly listening to the same bewildered old man that they heard on the radio all the way down? Honestly, it was one of the largest rallies that you could legally claim Alan Jones was responsible for inciting. It was almost as effective as his protest against windfarms, which I hear actually managed to stop the wind for a short time.

What a clear difference there is between the truckers' decent expression of democracy and the travesty that is Occupy Wall Street. Honestly, if you wanted to occupy Wall Street then maybe you should have gotten a job as a high-end stock trader.

I am not against the notion of social change per se. It is necessary, particularly when a king or queen passes away and a new era is ushered in. What I am against is artificial social change that leaves life better for some people but worse for others.

Let's put this in numbers. On a scale of quality, from one to ten, my life is a solid nine. Yours, I imagine, is at best a four. I have no problem with increasing your quality of life to a five, or perhaps even a six. But why should I have to drop to an eight? All I am asking for is a blueprint for radical social upheaval that leaves the status quo perfectly intact. This isn't just a preference, it's a necessity. Again, let's return to our numbers. If you're happily living your little four life as the four you are, to suddenly elevate as high as a six would seem like an incredible dream. But for me, to drop from the lofty heights of a nine down to the disgusting gutter of an eight would be a pain worse than any torture I could imagine, or recommend inflicting upon enemy combatants.

Here we get to the crux of the issue: equality feels oppressive to me. At times, I like to imagine myself as the late great King John of England being rudely forced into signing the Magna Carta. To the rebels howling at my door it must have come as a sweet surprise and a great improvement to their repulsive lives, but for me, being coerced into even the slightest concession and limitation of power would burn like fire.

If we wish to bridge the gaps in our society the Left have to admit that some of us are living better than the lives currently promised by equality, which would be unacceptable downgrade. We need a form of compensation for those who have the most to lose by sheer virtue of currently having the most.

What I'm proposing is a form of rich reparations. That is, you are allowed to increase your earnings and position in society provided that you compensate your more wealthy colleagues who are flabbergasted to now be seated at the same table as you. It could take the form of a simple tax or tithing, but it must go beyond purely financial restitution. All we are looking for is a better quality of life than these nouveau rich, or these newly-no-longer-desperately-poor.

What I'm proposing might sound like a call to reintroduce segregation but I would prefer to think of it as opening a VIP section of society. It's not that the regular club is bad, it's just that some of us have become accustomed to being one of an exclusive set in the champagne room and we plan to keep it that way.

Of course, when I propose this solution I'm asked by simpletons to explain exactly how the poor are meant to elevate themselves in a society not only stacked against them but also in a system where they now have to pay what money they do have to the upper class for the honour of their company. The solution is simple: they just need to show a little initiative. Pull themselves up by their bootstraps. Give it a go. Land a job as a CEO of an ASX200 company. It's not that hard, people.

That's why Australians hate it when these do-gooders (who are obsessed with doing good, mind you) push for higher tax rates on the wealthy.* Once again, this is class warfare which is particularly unconscionable since, as I have previously mentioned, we do not have class in this nation and thus the upper class are virtually unarmed in such conflict.

Far too often the Left try to pit the poor and rich against one another. This is absurd. Clearly they should be natural allies: the poor want more money. The rich have proven they know how to get more money. Perhaps if the poor just listened to the rich we wouldn't have inequality at all.

If we're all battlers then surely the wealthy are our champions. They've battled the hardest and won the most. We should not be taxing them, we should be praising them. They should be treated like the great Roman gladiators of old who won favour by murdering slaves in front of adoring crowds.

The simple fact is you cannot solve income inequality by taking money from the rich. It just doesn't work. That's why we've never tried

---

* This lobbying is pathetically constant, purely because it never ends up happening.

it. If it had promise we would have given it a shot but it clearly doesn't so we haven't. Think of it this way: if you take money from the rich and give it to the poor you simply end up swapping who is rich and who is poor. This is presumably the lesson learned by Robin Hood.

We constantly hear about the growing divide between the rich and the poor. But no one can articulate why exactly this is a problem. Let's look at it logically. The poor have, let's say, zero dollars. As the rich get richer, due to their superior genetics and dress sense, the gap will naturally increase between these two groups. That doesn't mean life is getting worse for the poor people. It's not like they can go into negative dollars!*

Still, apparently some of the nation's poor aren't satisfied with having no money, and do in fact want to enter into crushing debt by attempting to buy a home. For renters, home ownership is a childish obsession akin to wanting a cubbyhouse of your own to play in.†

It's ridiculous the importance we have imposed upon this boring basic necessity of shelter. Somehow, the symbol for inequality has become the simple, modest house. Apparently, we now hear, it is impossible for young people to own a home. Of course, the obvious answer is constantly ignored by these professional grievance merchants. The property market already has mechanisms to make owning your own home as simple as a Greens voter. The trick is to already have a home. Once you have a home you have wealth and equity. You can negatively gear or borrow from your mortgage. It really is that easy.

---

* That's a fun little joke but in reality they do tend to have hugely crippling debt. That's also a fun little joke, in a way.

† It's worth noting that my cubbyhouse was a small terrace in Potts Point that is now worth quite a nice sum.

Sure, people will complain that they do not already have a home and thus cannot get a second home but that's really their problem. They should have thought about this years ago. Right now is the worst possible time to be trying to buy a house. As they say, the early bird gets the worm and the stupid worm deserves to die.

All serious homeowners know that you should already have your house by now. Attempting to enter the property market at this stage is like playing musical chairs and deciding to not try and claim a chair until long after the music has stopped. In this case, the music stopped some time back in the late 1970s when music was still good.

The pity parties will claim that they were not born earlier but whose fault is that? It sounds to me like these layabouts decided to nap in the womb and now they're paying the price.

Beyond that, it's clearly not impossible! Hardly a month goes by without seeing a success story of an inspiring, hardworking youth bucking the trend and entering the housing market. We in the media rightly identify these people as shining beacons of hope by which the hideous moths of their generation can find their way. When you delve deeply into these articles they all have a commonality: at some period the inspirational stars of these articles were given a great deal of money or some kind of advantage such as not having to pay rent. It's a brilliant savings method and one I highly recommend for all young people.

And yet there are still caws from the jealous crows on the Left who are furious that they didn't think of the idea first. If they had the wherewithal to be given their own large sum of money without strict terms of a loan then we wouldn't be in this issue. Once again, it's their own short-sightedness that's costing them now.

Young couples wishing to enter the property market can simply ask their parents for the money for a deposit. If their parents lack the required funds then they can ask their parents and so on and so forth until the problem is solved.

There are means of getting more money! Millennials ignore this at their own peril. When was the last time you saw a millennial treasure hunter or bank robber? They're happy to complain but refuse to take action. It's typical.

Let me be clear here: I'm not arguing that young people should not be allowed to own property. Far from it. I'm merely claiming that property is an end goal. You need to work your way up to it. Attempting to enter the property market from nothing is going from zero to one hundred. Instead, you need to take it in steps. Live in a tent for a while. If you like the tent and can afford it, then upgrade to some kind of dog kennel. From the kennel you could find a suitable cubbyhouse and before you know it we're thirty years down the track and you have yourself a campervan with four flat tyres, which is for all intents and purposes a house.

It's unfair to say I'm opposed to making it easier for respectable youth to join the property market. If someone is of good character and worthy standing then we should do whatever is possible to give them some kind of run-down shack they can eventually die in. That's just good manners.

And even I can admit that acquiring property was easier in the olden days. Once upon a time, if you wanted a house all you had to do was wait for your mysterious uncle to pass away and then spend one night inside his mansion on the top of Corpse Hill. But when you talk to young people now you realise they clearly do not have the patience necessary to ignore the blood-curdling screams throughout the night. They want everything to be perfect instantly and are unwilling to put up with the occasional moving painting or bleeding wall.

But if someone does have the right attitude I believe we should find ways to assist them, which is why I have worked out the following solutions.

Outdoor Provisions Program: The 'permanently camping' approach

We need alternatives to housing. What better method than to issue every young person in Australia with a simple, durable tent, allowing them to turn any public park into their permanent home. This way, no one is locked out of the market. They'll all be enjoying luxurious nights under the stars.

Of course, it would be a waste of money for the government to pay for these tents, so reimbursement will be acquired by forcibly selling off the possessions of the youths until the tent is fully costed. There will also be fees for continuing occupation of the tent. Failure to pay will result in the confiscation of said tent. Further restrictions will prevent the youth from using the generously provided equipment to create any kind of tent embassy to push for political change.

And before anyone dares say it, any suggestion that this is nothing more than a attempt to bolster my failing military supplies chain is completely unfounded. I'll have you know we've found an extremely lucrative revenue stream selling expired rations to local orphanages, thank you very much.

Deceased Estate Occupation: The 'better off dead' approach

We need intergenerational compromise. While I do not believe it is right to force the elderly to give up their properties to the youth, I do think it would be pertinent to open up any deceased estates for twenty-four hours to a 'might is right' situation, wherein anyone capable of capturing and holding the disputed territory would be considered the rightful owner from this point forward. This will temporarily quiet the millennial hordes by delivering false hope that boomers will die. Of course we won't, but let them dream for a while.

The Rural Initiative: Rack off for your own good

Now we come to my permanent solution to the housing crisis.

Part of the so-called housing affordability crisis is that everyone wants to move into the inner city. The far Left youth, terrified of Real Australia, are all constantly attempting to run into the city at once, like the Three Stooges getting stuck in a doorway.

They think that just because everywhere they work, learn and play is in the city that it's necessary to live close to it. Garbage. It is entirely reasonable for young people to live four or five hours from the city and commute every day. Not only would this raise revenue for the government through train tickets (and even better, fines for a lack of train ticket), it would give young people a chance to see more of this great nation and open up more than a few tables at my local cafe of a weekend.

Not everyone can live in the city and not everyone should. The Australian Bureau of Statistics likes to claim that 66 per cent of all Australians live in a capital city as of 2013 and they expect that number to increase to 72 per cent by 2053. These are shocking numbers. Personally, I was stunned to discover that the vast majority of the citizens of this nation are not Real Australians.

It is imperative for the longevity of this nation that we find ways to encourage young people to move out into wider Australia. Part of the job can be done via the media through programs that show off the beauty of our nation's heart, such as *Wolf Creek*. But the majority of the work will need to be much more hands-on.

I propose we take all the unsatisfied renters and people desperate to enter the property market, gather them together, and dump them in an unspecified location in central Australia, somewhere near where they used to do all that nuclear testing.

From there three scenarios could arise, all with their own unique benefits:

1 The group forms their own society, foraging for whatever materials they can find until they can slowly build a new city. This is an ideal scenario, both as a solution to the housing crisis and for establishing a location to which we can send undesirables.

2 The group forms their own society, attempt to forage whatever materials they can, fail miserably, and die slowly in the desert. This will decrease housing demand and solve the crisis.

3 The abandoned nuclear materials somehow trigger the mutation of a dormant gene within the group, turning them into a battalion of super-soldiers which we can use to conquer new lands, thereby solving the housing crisis.

There really are no downsides to this proposal and it makes sense that I was awarded the Order of Australia for my efforts, even if it was a private ceremony held by my family without the explicit endorsement of the Australian government.

5 | Welfare is Anything But, Well, Fair

'Those with their hands out will soon have their hands up, as they are arrested for being openly poor.'

—PETER CHUDD, PROFOUNDLY

What's the most dangerous Australian animal?

Is it the great white shark?* Is it the crocodile? Perhaps it's something once considered mythical, like the yowie, the Blue Mountains panther or the Reasonable Greens Voter.

No, it's none of these things. It's very much real. It's present. It walks amongst us.

It's the Dole Bludger.

Yes, the dole bludger is the most dangerous animal known to Australia. A great white shark destroys a person but the dole bludger destroys a society. But still, whenever you propose a cull of these vile creatures the animal rights groups get up in arms about it. Fortunately for us, the dole bludger is an endangered species: we're in the midst of a budget crisis so we finally have carte blanche to remove a few undesirables under the guise of fiscal security.

---

* Yes, the shark is GREAT and WHITE. I will not take this back.

Whenever there are cuts to be made, all heads turn towards welfare. This is partly because our nation's welfare system is incredibly bloated* and there's a lot of hay to be made by picking on the less fortunate, but it's also quite savvy politically. The vast majority are already disenfranchised, so the risk of losing votes is fairly low. Add to this the limited capacity for political organising and you're already onto a winner. The best part is, in the event that you're cutting funding to vital services, these people will be too busy trying to keep their fragile lives together in any way, shape or form that they simply will not have time to protest. That's successful policy-making.

Welfare reform may not be popular but it is a necessary move. At some point we have to face that our society cannot take care of everyone—or at least, we can but have specifically chosen not to do so.

The problem, as far as I can see it, is that welfare is going to the wrong people. Welfare should go to the people who have proven themselves to be the most industrious and successful in our society. It should go to the best of us, as a reward for a good job well done. Instead, welfare is wasted on people who do nothing but collect free money and use it to pay for their boutique housing and artisanal medication.

The abuse of our welfare system is endemic and the problem begins at implementation. It's far too easy for these people to apply for handouts nowadays. The process is so simple it's shocking: while true Australians head off for a hard day of honest work, these dole bludgers are dropping into the office of some quack doctor to get a note saying that they're allergic to the sweat of their brow. This note is then taken to the local Centrelink office where the bludger is asked to fill in a simple form. This part of the process can take some weeks as filling in a sheet of paper is considered by many to be almost work. Once all the paperwork

---

* I will NOT apologise for body-shaming our welfare system.

is sorted, the bludger is assigned a hardworking taxpayer, who is then bled absolutely dry funding the bludger's lifestyle of video games, fast food and light ISIS recruitment.

We need to get these bludgers back into the workforce. The time for soft talk is over. Treasurer Scott Morrison was on the right track when he considered delaying payments to students for the first six months. Starve them out, I say. It's a brilliant move that I learned while hunting rabbits at my local petting zoo.

Young people lack the willpower to work of their own volition. Medical professionals have shown me detailed patient histories of millennials whose vital organs shut down when exposed to employment. This poses a medical challenge, as it's harder to simply chain them up and force them to work, as I would prefer. It's necessary, therefore, to tempt them into work with the promise of food and shelter or, better yet, goad them with the fear of an electric shock.[*]

This is also why I supported Morrison's PaTH program, and not just because its daring use of improper capitals set my heart aflutter. The program proposed to take many of the concepts from Tony Abbott's Green Army, including recruiting youth workers, and the brilliant cost-saver of barely paying them, and do away with the useless environmental elements.[†]

It was widely criticised by the hysterical Left when it was revealed that those undertaking the program would only be earning four dollars per hour for their work, but it's important to note that this is on top

---

[*]   You can buy my branded shock-collars for your troublesome teen online now.

[†]   I must admit, I was an ardent supporter of the Green Army back when I believed it was a program to use military force to finally rid us of Leftists. What a waste of a perfectly good program name.

of their welfare payments, so they aren't being criminally underpaid, just underpaid the regular amount.

At the very least, it gets people back into work. My heart breaks when I think about all the wasted potential in our society. There are so many people sitting about on their couches who could be better used as a perfectly adequate fuel source to power our mining equipment. Of course, there were protests but this is to be expected and fortunately, being so unused to work, the demonstrators were soon tuckered out and easily bundled into vans to be taken to the recruitment centres.

Morrison was right when he divided our society into the 'taxed' and the 'taxed-nots'. You know the groups all too well. There are the hard workers, the lifters, you and me, on the frontline of the workforce, giving everything we've got every single day from precisely 9 a.m. till exactly 5 p.m. We're the taxed. We're the lifeblood of this economy. We pay for the schools, the roads, the hospitals. Honestly, whenever someone is horribly injured these days they should thank their lucky stars that I've bought them an ambulance, a road, a hospital and, if it comes down to it, a crematorium.

Then you have the taxed-nots.

Please, at this moment, imagine that I have paused to spit on the ground again and again until it triggers a small coughing fit and I slip on the newly made puddle at my feet, crashing headfirst into the ground and shattering my skull on the concrete.

The taxed-nots. The bludgers. This sewer-filth exists in a symbiotic relationship with left-wing guilt that helps the man lying in the gutter rather than the more efficient move of just leaving him for the street-sweeper. Honestly, these are the kind of people who believe that pausing in the middle of a race to help your fallen opponent makes you both heroes, when the timesheet clearly shows it makes you both losers. The Left love to crow that society is judged by how it treats its most vulnerable members but I would like to add that lions judge herds of gazelles by their most vulnerable members. Once again, it's clear that society operates at its peak when it most resembles a bloodthirsty lion on the prowl.

In my opinion, the only people who should get away with not paying tax are the small, family-run international conglomerates whose very presence in our small nation is thanks enough for me. I do not require their money. Far from being satisfied with paying nothing, however, this younger generation expects money to constantly flow to them without any repercussions, as if it were coal! The current generation has been raised to expect government handouts as if they were party to some sort of social contract just by the very grace of being alive!

Know this: your government doesn't owe you anything. People don't pay taxes so they can get an equal amount out of their society. You pay your taxes because the government owns all the tanks and they will come for you if you don't.* With all the money pissed away in the welfare system it's surprising we can find any left over for essential purchases like twelve billion dollars on Joint Strike Fighters. We need to get our priorities straight.

Not too long ago the *Daily Telegraph* was criticised for daring to oppose this welfare culture. Unafraid, the paper boldly published a front page comparing the number of people on a disability support pension to our nation's war wounded. It was a brilliant cover, unswayed by political correctness, or the fact that a good number of the people on a disability support pension could well have been wounded defending our nation. They didn't opt for the easy way out by acknowledging that Australia's population has tripled since the war, making a straight comparison of numbers completely worthless. They had a higher purpose.

---

* For the moment we'll ignore the abhorrent injustice preventing me from owning a tank.

The *Daily Telegraph* went beyond these basic assumptions and decided that there is absolutely no excuse for the ballooning rise in disability support pension (DSP) claimants, particularly if you discount the increased restrictions on Newstart that were put in place specifically because of pressure on welfare payments, forcing a large number of people to switch to the DSP due to not meeting minimum health standards. This is the kind of insightful journalism that looks beyond boring facts to get to the real heart of their opinion of what's happening.

The reason behind the exponential rise in welfare payments is becoming all too clear, with people expecting handouts for everything from the need to survive to even requiring it to strive for a better quality of life. And most shocking of all is the government's plan to add to this egregious waste by implementing paid domestic violence leave. I'm aware that domestic violence is an epidemic within our society but that doesn't mean we have to do anything about it.

As a matter of principle, I do not agree with any leave. In my opinion, you get plenty of sick leave the day you die from an easily treatable cancer. It's my belief that we made a mistake shortening the workday to eight hours in the first place. True workers know their shift is finished for the day when they are no longer physically capable of movement.

Now we're being forced to decide which we believe is more important: a woman's life, or the proper and efficient allocation and categorisation of annual leave in a workplace agreement. Frankly, I don't know.

Personally, I share the concerns of my colleague Miranda Devine who worried that these measures will lead to people, as she put it, 'chucking a divvie'. Other people may have found her remarks disgusting and bizarre but it's plain common sense. Again, it hasn't happened yet, but that we can imagine it happening at all is shocking. Miranda is right to wonder, given the opportunity, if people will choose to undergo the lasting trauma of physical and emotional violence, and then up-end their entire world in a desperate attempt to preserve their lives, just to have an extra day off. If you had floated this possibility to me a year ago I'd have considered it absolute nonsense. So much can change within a year.

This is why it's so understandable that Senator Mathias Cormann is considering the deleterious effect these measures could have on the economy. You know his concerns must be serious because he's managed to maintain them despite reports indicating the plan would have a minimal economic effect. Estimates by the Australia Institute's Centre for Future Work suggest that only about one and a half per cent of women would use the leave in any given year but that's still too many. I believe it's important to focus on the massive impact I've decided it will have on our economy, at the very least because it keeps us from focusing on the fact that one and a half per cent of people in any given year will need to seek emergency leave due to this epidemic.

Cormann was adamant, in the face of contradictory evidence from loony Lefty economists, that implementation of domestic violence leave could affect our competitiveness in the global market. Once again, Cormann displayed his prophetic ability to look beyond the facts of the issue, showing that this is less about the economic outlook per se and more about our foreign business partners looking down on us if they know we put women's lives ahead of profits.

And it's just another example of a problem plaguing the whole system, which is that our welfare is being disproportionately wasted on the needy. We need to ask ourselves whether the goal of our society is to prop up every single person so that they may reach their full potential and contribute, or if it's about the much more noble goal of sifting through society and sorting out the winners and losers of capitalism.

Sure, when I see someone struggling to survive I think, 'There but for the grace of God go I,' but then I realise I must have the grace of God on my side. Clearly I am favoured by the Lord. And I ask myself, what would my Lord and Saviour prefer I do: help the needy, or just really enjoy the advantages I have been granted? I think the answer is pretty obvious. Were I to pass on my wealth to anyone else it would be like re-gifting. Rude!

The simple fact of the matter is we cannot afford the system as it stands. Or more precisely, we are choosing not to afford the system as it stands. This is why I was such an ardent supporter of Centrelink's Robo-Debt system that calculated exactly what you owed the government for its kind clemency in permitting your survival. Of course, the Left complained when people were being billed for debts they never accrued, and when these mistakes were deliberately left uncorrected as the system expanded to specifically target more vulnerable groups such as the elderly and disabled.

It's disingenuous to pretend this wasn't a perfectly logical decision. If a system is under fire then you *should* be attacking the most disenfranchised, since they're the least likely to be able to adequately defend themselves. It's one of the easiest ways to get away with a nefarious plan that we've ever known.

Is this fair? Yes, definitely. Thank you for asking.

It was a brilliantly aggressive move in what is, make no mistake, a war against people selfishly trying to survive on my money.* We're being exploited and we need to do something about it. Perhaps it's true that, if we try to crack down on the minority using the welfare system for their own advantage, innocent people desperately in need would suffer. All I'm saying is, I've made my peace with this. I'm prepared to take on this burden and stay steadfast to my beliefs—unless, of course,

---

* Even my own lovely, hirsute boy Rand would not receive formula as a toddler without performing at least an hour of physical labour.

any kind of hardship ever befalls me. If that happens, I'll be in the Centrelink line so fast it will make your head spin.

And you'd better give me what I need.

I signed a social contract.

6

The Only Thing Warming the World is the Hot Air from Environmentalists

'Even if the Earth was warming would that not just be further proof of the excellent heating potential of coal? What a magnificent rock.'

—PETER CHUDD, ERUDITELY

Global warming is the single greatest scam played on the world and I say this as a man who has lost tens of thousands of dollars unselfishly trying to help Nigerian royalty reclaim their rightful throne.

That the scientific community would dare conspire to manipulate data from all around the world with thousands upon thousands of complicit scientists is so shocking that you could hardly believe it was possible, were it not true. The conspiracy is so far-reaching, complex and detailed that it reads like nonsensical fiction, the kind of borderline delusion you would usually find scrawled on the back of the door in a public bathroom.

People ask me how I'm so confident global warming is a hoax and I always tell them the same thing: first, thank you for noticing my confidence. I've been trying this new thing where I wear a completely new pair of socks every day as a little gift from me to me and it's really helped my self-esteem. Then I say, it's all about certainty. I am certain that global warming is a hoax so therefore it must be.

I'm a deeply intelligent, innovative and remarkably insightful thinker. It's highly unlikely that I would be on the wrong side of an issue. It's even more unlikely that there would be a general consensus that everyone could see that I couldn't accept. Therefore, this must be a hoax. If there truly was a litany of compelling evidence then I would have seen it and accepted it. As it stands, not only have I not seen this evidence, I have gone out of my way to avoid it.

For me, it all comes down to one telling gap of knowledge: if the fact of global warming is so patently obvious then why am I incapable of accepting it? So far, no scientist has been able to answer this for me. Until one does, I will not be buying into their conspiracy.

This Global Warming Hysteria™ is typical of the Left, who desperately want to shame the general public for participating in the Industrial Revolution.* Of course, the Industrial Revolution was the greatest thing to ever happen to Western civilisation. At last, the common man was able to get off the farm and go to work in a factory—and he could bring his children!

It was a golden age. There were no handouts or welfare back then. You just worked hard in demanding and unsafe conditions until you were involved in an industrial accident and then took your rightful place rotting in the gutter alongside your co-workers. This was long before the corrupt unions got their hands on the industry and ruined labour for everyone.

It's easy to see how this paradise became a target for the Left in their attempts to eliminate all records of hard work being done. The

---

*	According to these alarmists, steam power is as an act of violence perpetrated against water.

scam is brilliant in its simplicity. Everything we do is wrong! You can't drive your car, fly a plane, light a tyre fire, throw a television in a lake, open a coal mine or shoot at an unarmed person without contributing to global warming. And it all comes down to a magical invisible gas. Likely story.

Frankly, the notion that greenhouse gases could possibly change the temperature of our Earth is absurd. It's the worst kind of scaremongering! Now, I do not claim to be an atmosphere expert. As far as I am concerned any airspace not taken up by a fighter jet is a waste and potentially jeopardising our national security. Still, in my considered opinion, global warming just doesn't seem feasible. It seems much more likely that we could pump exhaust from our factories, vehicles and animals fairly consistently for hundreds of years without any negative consequences.

Each day, I spend about half an hour sitting with my face directly in front of my car's exhaust and it has never done me any harm. If anything, it's my favourite part of the day. The auto-exfoliation routine has been wonderful for giving my skin that much desired light-grey sheen.

We cannot trust the information from NASA. The data is corrupted. It is a political organisation with an inherent bias towards cataclysmic events as it helps its funding targets. We saw this happen in the 1960s when a small group of NASA scientists convinced child-president John F. Kennedy that the moon was going to fall to earth unless they went up there and lashed it to the sun.

What shocks me is just how brazenly these various climate-monitoring stations around the world uphold the conspiracy. If they aren't in cahoots then please explain to me how all of their measurements are consistent across the entire planet?

But governments around the world have bought in wholesale to this trick, wasting billions of dollars of taxpayers' money instead of making the responsible decision to wait and see if the world really is ending and then act.

Here's the terrible secret: the boffins in the CSIRO want global warming to be real because all climatologists secretly pray for death. It's understandable, considering their lives. That's the motivation behind all of this.

It seems deeply malicious and unsavoury but some time ago these scientists realised that there is money to be made from the apocalypse. Nothing moves funding like the prospect of the imminent end of humanity.

Now, regular listeners to my radio show and podcast will know that I eagerly await death. When my time comes I will not slowly slip into the good night, I will leave this world as screaming, bloody and nude as I entered it. But even I cannot comprehend the sadism that is necessary to inflict these lies on the global community.

It's bizarre to me to see the warmists claim that humans are responsible for climate change. For one, it's the only time I've ever seen this lot take responsibility for anything! The last time we had a major climate event of the same magnitude was the Ice Age. Do these warmists truly expect us to believe that the Ice Age was caused by humans? They played a minor role, if any: the main story was clearly driven by the Italian mammoth, the rude cat and the weasel with the learning difficulty.

The Earth moves in these cycles naturally. Sometimes it gets progressively colder over the course of about 10,000 years. Sometimes it gets incrementally hotter over the course of 150 years. We should not demonise the Earth's current warming cycle for its efficiency.

We're not saying that the Earth isn't slowly becoming uninhabitable. We're just saying that we aren't to blame for it beginning and even if we did contribute to the problem, it wasn't significant enough to justify having to do anything about it. It's exactly the same excuse I give for not cleaning up after a party.

Even if it were true that human beings were affecting our climate, why should this be considered a bad thing? No other civilisation can claim to have had such a profound effect on their planet. Sure, the pyramids are impressive but in a sense they're also embarrassingly dormant after thousands of years, reminding everyone that that empire fell. When we leave the Earth, we're taking everyone else with us. That's power. It's better to burn out than to fade away.

Rabid millennials try and paint this whole situation as an embarrassing failure of the boomer generation. They try to claim that we are short-sighted and sacrificing their futures—I know, how sweet that they actually believe they have futures.

All the same, this is typical of the intergenerational war we're seeing between the disrespectful youth and the faultless, wise elders. From the outside, boomers and millennials have an awful lot in common: they're both frighteningly large voting bases, they both have nothing but disdain for gen X-ers, and they both consider themselves to be the greatest generation that ever lived, despite having significantly more proud Nazis than any other time around them.

Unfortunately, that's where the similarities end. The attitude of this new generation could not be further from ours. While we boomers are forthright, millennials are unwilling to compromise. While we demand immediate results, they are recklessly impatient. While we understand our worth, they are obscenely demanding.

When I was a kid we didn't complain about the job market collapsing, we just went out and got a job. We didn't piss and moan about a complete lack of affordable housing, we just bought an affordable house. We didn't complain night and day about racism and sexism, we politely ignored it. This societal ideal of carrying on without making a fuss no matter how awful things were led to some of the most prosperous times our nation has ever known and only a couple of scandals within major institutions and beloved television programs.

When I was growing up we were taught to respect our elders. We were taught that by our elders, actually. They were taught it by theirs and so on and so forth. But these days we have to ask ourselves, what does respect look like? What does respect mean? To me, the answer is patently obvious. Respect is unconditional loyalty. The world you see before you was built by your elders and to attempt to improve it is disrespectful to their work.

Yet you see this new generation questioning our decisions at every turn! Their lack of trust is astounding. It's as if they've seen us work directly against their interests at every opportunity and no longer believe we're doing it for their own good! The youth of this nation believe that we're slowly destroying the planet through our mindless selfishness and inexplicable stupidity. How wrong they are to underestimate us. As right-thinking Australians know, the unwillingness to address concerns relating to the destruction of the natural world is not a blind spot, it's a warning: nothing helps you demonstrate your dominance over someone else like destroying the planet they live on. If you happen to also live on it then that's bad luck—but at least you weren't planning to be there long.

For too long millennials have tried to ignore their elders and force us into retirement or perhaps our graves. It became very clear to me that there's only one right way to fight back and that was to slowly and methodically destroy the Great Barrier Reef. I put a notch in my belt every time a writer under thirty criticises one of my articles as poorly researched and full of typos, or someone emails me an offensive gif in which my face has been crudely photoshopped onto a basketball being dunked by LeBron James. Then, when I'm next on the coast, I count my notches and buy that many bottles of bleach to pour directly onto the Great Barrier Reef. This is my own form of direct activism and vengeance.

The Leftist media scream that the Great Barrier Reef is a natural wonder, and that I am taking it for granted with no regard for the future when it isn't around. To this I wittily raise an eyebrow and say, 'You mean I'm treating it the way you treat the greatest generation?' I'm not exaggerating, dear readers, when I tell you that this answer is so brilliantly succinct that it has caused three of my detractors to be hospitalised overnight.

Still, even if this global warming narrative is true, the constant fear-mongering clouds the many positives. We hear so much about rising sea levels but so little about all the opportunities in new waterfront property. We hear about bushfire season stretching on indefinitely but never about finally returning to the endless summers of our youth. We are constantly bombarded with images of polar bears floating on solitary ice caps headed out to sea, as if that's a terrible outcome of global warming. But when you look a little deeper, you realise that that is actually just incredibly cute and would make a heartwarming Coca-Cola commercial one Christmas.

Also, it's a bear. To hell with bears. Given the chance, a bear would kill me in a heartbeat.* If I just happen to land the first blow through a lack of climate action, then so be it.

My opinions on the supposed 'cracking of Antarctica' are along the same lines. Exactly what has the massive ice shelf ever done for me? If I want ice I press the button on my fridge and it appears. I do not need Antarctica and I do not want Antarctica.

The hysterical Lefties beg us to think of the future and their children and their grandchildren, as if imagining the feral spawn of these goblins would make me inclined to want to save the Earth instead of accelerating its decline. This isn't a crisis, it's an opportunity! They are

---

* At least, it would try.

desperate to frighten us into submission with their doomsaying but what they don't understand is that what they consider a hideous apocalypse, I call a beautiful summer's day.

A longer bushfire season would also allow further chances to show true blue Australian heroism. We will no longer have to wait until the last few months of the year to celebrate the wonderful work of the rural firefighters; in this brave future, our patriots will be appreciated every day of the year.

Furthermore, fewer Pacific Islands will not simply make mapmaking considerably easier, it will also greatly help our immigration program. We'll no longer be frozen with indecision when trying to choose which island to next approach to resettle refugees: it'll be the only island still technically inhabitable.

Climate believers have shuddered in fright at my brave stance. They know the jig is up. You can already see them capitulating. They're afraid to use the term 'global warming' anymore after I thoroughly embarrassed them all by pointing out that on some days it was actually very cold, not hot at all. Sure, they may claim that 'climate change' more accurately encompasses the extremes on both ends of the spectrum, or that the term 'global warming' is offensive to thermometers, or whatever, but we know the truth. I stared them down and they blinked first.

If you're wondering how I can be so perceptive, calm and collected in the face of such hysteria, the answer is that I've seen it all before. A decade ago the warmists were all rendered catatonic by the confected crisis of the hole in the ozone layer. If you, like me, thought the 'O-zone' was just another feminist term for genitalia, this panic made absolutely no sense. But apparently it was another climate catastrophe waiting to happen. According to that little conspiracy, CFCs in aerosols were going to puncture a hole in our atmosphere, sucking us all into space. Again, how convenient for a group with no regard for personal hygiene to discover that using deodorant was an immoral activity. I would hardly be surprised if in a few years they're all in a flap about some new environmental issue that can only be solved by having unprotected sex while listening to the John Butler Trio.

I mean, honestly, when you see some of the things these sheep genuinely believe will one day occur, well, you'd laugh if you weren't already doubled over crying for unrelated reasons. The following are just some of the predictions made by warming alarmist Tim Flannery:

- Australia's dams will never be full again unless we all jump in at the same time.
- All ice will catch fire.
- It will never rain again.
- Sea levels will rise so high that even waves will be underwater.
- Dogs will shed all their fur to deal with extreme heat.
- The jumper industry will go entirely bankrupt.
- Eggs will cook inside chickens.

Of course, there's a reason the laughable Leftists are pursuing this agenda with such fervour and it's all too obvious: they're already planning to profit from the so-called energy crisis with their beloved renewables.

By the way, before we go any further can we just note that coal is also a renewable energy. Coal allows life to be sustained on Earth. This life will eventually die, rejoin the Earth's surface and be slowly compressed into coal again. Perfectly renewable. Unsurprisingly, my opponents are utterly incapable of seeing reason and in doing so expose their agenda. They're only happy supporting *their* renewables.

Solar power is perhaps the most pathetic vice of the Left. These children of the sun believe that since they have found a way to do nothing but lie about in the sun all day and somehow get by, that our entire society should do the same. There are so many flaws with solar power it's hard to fathom how we even got to this point. First and foremost, the majority of energy is used at night. Unless you can get your solar power from the moon you're out of luck, buddy. If we cannot draw power from the moon, the obvious next question is how do we store the power from the sun? You'd think it would be as easy as warming yourself up and doing your best to not radiate away any heat but that has thus far proven extremely difficult.

Even if we manage to do this, do we not run the risk of using up all the energy from the sun? Isn't that how we got the moon in the first place? I'll check with Ross Cameron and get back to you.

Still, it doesn't end there. Not satisfied with stealing the light, these Leftists also want the air we breathe! Of course, I am talking about the scourge of the wind farm, which have long been the pet of environmental warriors hell-bent on backing whatever new technology they believe will most effectively destroy our economy. These wind farms hold none of the innate beauty of an open-cut coal mine. Flying over a coal mine is like having a peek through those books you had as children which showed cross-sections of ships and pyramids—except with the Earth. Mines are opportunities for an education on the crust of our planet and how it is being extracted for the goodness of humanity.

While questions remain over whether wind farms are capable of supporting the electricity grid of a major city, one fact remains plainly true: wind farms are ugly. Who cares how much energy they generate? These hideous bastards make me absolutely sick every time I do the drive from Sydney to Canberra. If you've never had the displeasure, allow me to describe the monsters. Wind farms tend to stand atop otherwise idyllic hillsides, blighting the picturesque countryside. They resemble a child's pinwheel toy, provided the child had an affinity for Stanley Kubrick design aesthetics and loved anything alabaster white.* Their

_____

*   See, Rand! I told you I'd reference you! Love you, buddy.

haunting presence dangles over the pasture like the sword of Damocles, a frightening shadow of rotating blades projected onto the green grass.

(One can only imagine what the humble cow thinks of this monstrosity. Far be it from me to claim to know what happens in the mind of the beautiful milk beast but, were I a cow, having a rotating blade hanging above my head could be a most unnerving experience indeed! When I muse on it further I can imagine that, yes, given time I might become used to them and, even, yes, had I been born after their installation I could see my cow-self worshipping the rotors as if they were gods. Perhaps then when the time came to be sent to the abattoir my last moments would be utterly peaceful as I would believe I were about to meet with my Lord. In a way, I suppose I'd even be correct. But I digress.)

This would hardly be an issue if being pointless and ugly were the only crimes of wind farms. Which radio presenter is not guilty of the same? No, the real trauma of wind farms comes from an illness so pernicious that not even medical research can find any evidence that it exists. I'm talking about wind turbine syndrome—another issue the Leftists are desperate to sweep under the flokati rug in their yurts.

When I first heard reports of this illness I loaded up on food and ammunition and headed to my holiday bomb shelter. It took my lovely producer four hours to assure me that the syndrome did not actually turn people into wind turbines. That said, it has never been sufficiently disproven.

As it turns out, the horrifying effects of wind turbine syndrome are much more subtle. The rotation of the wind turbine rotor emits a low constant rumbling sound, not unlike the one I make on my morning radio show to remind guests who's the alpha dog.* This 'infrasound' is

---

* It's me. I am the Alpha Dog and the Omega Dog.

so damaging it can travel over great distances, through walls and into homes, even when all records show that the wind turbine wasn't even operational when the symptoms were felt.

To this end, I call on the government to cut down any wind turbine caught making infrasound noise as a show of force and warning to all other renewable energies.

Beyond this, we need to start thinking long term! No one is asking what happens when we run out of wind. No one is questioning whether these wind farms will suddenly develop a taste for human flesh and wander the Earth in a green-energy inspired remake of *The Day of the Triffids*. Or what happens if a bird hits one of the rotors? I'm not a wind-rotor technician but if the energy is distributed from the blades it's not impossible that the bird could attain the powers of wind energy and we'd find ourselves under attack by a furious bird with an abundance of energy and the ability to summon cyclones at will.

The harm caused by reliance on renewable energy is readily apparent. In 2016 and 2017 we saw the entire South Australian electricity grid go dark overnight, and while this wasn't directly the fault of renewable energy, the indisputable fact that we can try to blame it on renewable energy is still troubling. These rolling blackouts sent shivers through the renewable energy establishment when they realised they were responsible, even if they weren't. One could only imagine the horror of such a disaster occurring when renewables actually were responsible. Is it worth the risk? I'd say not.

Environmentalists have tried to claim that it makes no sense to hold renewables accountable for an issue with which they had no involvement but I dispute this interpretation. It's not nonsensical to blame renewables; it is actually very easy, good and cool.

It's not as if the eco-warriors are entirely blameless themselves. This is the same petulant crew who accuse coal of everything from destroying the planet to providing the soot necessary for blackface. Australia has been so seduced by the notion that coal is evil we forget the wonderful things it has done for our nation. We forget the achievements made by our mum and dad open-cut coal mine owners. It's easy to paint the modern mine companies as oversized corporate villains but you must remember that all business is small business. Behind every multibillion-dollar mining operation is a family gathered around the kitchen table, struggling to make ends meet, saving every cent to put towards their campaign to strip-mine a national park.

Without coal we would have never had the delightful singing chimney sweep. Then what would Dickens have written about? That's the grim reality we're considering here: a world without stories romanticising child labour in the early Industrial Revolution. Without these classics of the English language the vast majority of people would never have learned just how much fun poverty can be.

Those on the Left love to claim righteous indignation whenever a mining operation is forced to improve a section of nature—probably because the idea of something that was once placid and useless becoming useful and worthwhile makes them feel guilty about their own lives. Frankly, I don't buy the notion that only the environmentalists care about the environment. Those of us who love and appreciate good rock coal understand that nature goes beyond the surface. These Green types talking about trees and native species have a facile and jejune understanding of the natural world; they completely fail to appreciate the hidden beauty of the Earth's mantle. By digging into the crust of the Earth we are granted the chance to be awed by the lesser-seen elements of nature. What environmentalists consider an attack on our natural world is nothing more than a considered appreciation of the lithosphere, asthenosphere and the continental crust.

Their insanity works against their own worldview! The truly progressive would understand that coal itself is an animal, when viewed outside the construct of time. Each metric tonne of coal exported overseas can be considered akin to a dinosaur fossil being loaned to another nation's museums or, in this case, burned for fuel. Even the Left's own beloved science rejects their backwards world-view: as any scientist will tell you, to attack coal is to fat-shame a diamond.

And then consider this: coal is carbon and we're carbon-based life forms. Perhaps the only way we can possibly understand the rabid hatred towards coal is as a symptom of the endemic self-hatred of the Left. This is not to say that their self-hatred isn't justified. If anything, it saves me a great deal of time I would otherwise have to spend hating them myself. It does neatly explain the situation though. Obviously those across the aisle see themselves in coal and therefore want it to be eliminated from the Earth. I would parry this notion thus: coal is a great deal more useful than the Left, though perhaps not as fun to burn for fuel.

Putting aside the environment and employment benefits, the cultural impact of coal is unparalleled. There is a reason Santa Claus gives naughty children coal. What Santa understands and the ludicrous Left do not is that coal means opportunity. If just one of those children has a drop of initiative in their blood they'll use that coal to power a factory, or perhaps on-sell it to China and use the proceeds to fund their start-up.

Coal fuels this nation. Always has, always will. The mining boom is not over until we say it's over. It's the duty of every good and patriotic Australian to find a new and innovative way to sell coal to foreign markets. If you cannot sell coal as an energy resource then sell it as a paperweight. Market it as a cheap and effective way to pave your driveway. Start a business selling custom-made pitch-black sandpits, a wonderfully enjoyable novelty that will provide fun for the whole family until respiratory problems force everyone to go indoors.

We need to ask ourselves how we can incorporate more coal into our daily lives. Whether it's adding an exotic flavour to your Boost Juice or simply as a rock to hurl during a riot, there's always space for more coal. This is the change I'd like to see in the world.

Perhaps one day, far in the future, my beautiful and powerful grand-children will order one of their generals to fetch them a copy of this book. Upon reading it, they will be aghast that people once entertained the notion of a warming globe. They will enter my cryogenic chamber, take a knee in front of my frozen body and thank me for not wasting important government funds stopping pollution or finding renewable energy sources. And then they will place their armour back on and head into the heart of the wasteland in search of the last drops of oil.

Unless I'm wrong and we all die—but I suppose at that stage it won't matter anyway.

7 | Who Comes to this Country and the Circumstances in which they are Imprisoned

'For those who've come across the seas, you should have listened to me in the first place when I told you to stay home.'
—PETER CHUDD, FURIOUSLY

Globalisation is one of the great achievements of humanity.

Thanks to the technological developments of our time, the entire planet has shrunk.* Nowadays there is free travel of products across the globe. We have new markets for exports and new options for imports. Perhaps this very book will be sold to some shepherd in a far-off land who, for the first time, will be able to experience the home-grown common sense that we here take for granted.

Unfortunately, with the incredible ability to move products comes the terrible possibility of moving people. This would be fine if we were just shipping members of the extremist Left to North Korea so that they'd finally have something worthwhile to complain about—but sadly this is a two-way street and people are now able to easily enter our great country.

---

* This is not to endorse Tim Flannery's prediction that global warming will shrink the Earth in a way similar to putting a woollen jumper in the dryer.

For too long we've sat on our hands while foreigners dared to come to this country to selfishly make a better life for themselves. What impertinence. You get the life that you're given and you're grateful for it. To strive for better is pure greed.

It's easy to act as if we don't really have a problem when you consider such small numbers of people are coming here amidst a massive international humanitarian crisis but it's a slippery slope. Once we let one person in, we let in ten and then twenty until eventually we have the entire population of this planet all crammed onto the same Melbourne tram.

Sure, we can say that we're only experiencing a fraction of the problem of European nations but that's scary in and of itself because I do not fully remember how to do fractions.

And who can blame them for flooding in when we made it so easy?* The majority of Australians think border security is nothing more than an entertaining Channel 7 show about finding reasons to put British backpackers in prison. While this is an important aspect of our security it's merely the tip of the iceberg.

Border security is about protecting Australians. It's essential we understand what a dangerous age we live in. Time and time again we have seen attacks on our shores that, even when they aren't actually committed by terrorists, have certainly been blamed on terrorists by major politicians, sometimes live on air while the victims are still being treated. It may seem disturbing and a little rehearsed to see how quickly someone can act on false information and declare Islamic extremism responsible for a tragic attack, implicitly justifying bigotry against average Muslim people, but it shows how horrible the situation is that we're already so close to crossing this dangerous threshold once and for all. It's imperative we understand how frightening the threat is and do our

---

*   The answer is me. I can blame them and I do blame them.

absolute best to prevent it, even if it means destroying our free society before these terrorists get a chance.

For decades I've tried to strengthen Australia's borders but have been thwarted at every turn. My attempt to sue Rand McNally for publishing Australia on its world maps was thrown out of court. My mission to smash the bulb of every lighthouse so no one could find us only resulted in my own arrest. Even our very own Department of Tourism refused to publish my brilliantly devised campaign: 'Where the bloody hell are you? Good. Stay there.' It's becoming increasingly apparent that I'm the only one who truly cares about defending our borders. If I could, I would personally stand on Cape York with a musket and a spotlight repelling all comers.

Of course, the Left love to mock the government's attempts to defend our nation. They ridiculed its once wonderfully effective slogan, 'Stop the boats'. Even the term 'three-word slogan' has become an attack in the modern political climate, a sign of pure jealousy at the unparalleled success of the three-word slogan. The Left have to admit they were outplayed here. In fact, that's an understatement. A three-word slogan absolutely demolished the Australian Labor Party. Had we added a fourth word it just might have killed Anthony Albanese. We beat the Labor Party so badly that they capitulated and are the centre Right now.

But the success of 'Stop the boats' was merely the prelude. As far as marketing manoeuvres go, the follow-up, 'Deaths at sea', was the 'Got Milk?' of conservative border protection policy. It's akin to a beautiful pin in chess or even a beautiful pin in professional wrestling. Here's how it works: no matter what your opponent is proposing, you counter that they're actually revealing a longing for more deaths at sea. It's remarkable the variety of situations this move can counter, from the public knowing about military operations run in their name, to the public knowing which nations we are transporting refugees to, and even the conditions those refugees face. So versatile! The only limits are your imagination and the burning pain in your stomach telling you that you simply cannot go on like this forever.*

This gambit has worked so perfectly that you cannot so much as argue for air-conditioning in a tropical island prison without being blasted for wanting to personally drown children. We can go even further down the rabbit hole and realise that setting this as our dichotomy instantly makes everything else permissible. If someone is screaming from the pain of torture it's proof of life—a step better than drowning at sea. Someone languishing in a detention centre, devoid of hope and wishing for death is, in a purely Descartian sense, still alive and therefore our job has been well done. You can even have people die in your facility and spin it: at least they were dry when they died.

You would think this argument might backfire when someone realises that we're using previous tragic loss of life to excuse cruel punishment but again we are well defended on this front. You see, we may be cruelly exploiting these past tragedies but it's no worse than the cruel exploitation caused by people smugglers. If you disagree, you must love drownings.

This is what activists don't understand.† They believe that when images and stories from these camps come out, we will be shut down by the goodness in human hearts. Unfortunately, this kind of moral activism is more effective for boycotts of small businesses with bizarre hiring practices than large-scale government-funded operations with bipartisan support.

In reality, the exposure of our cruelty further helps our cause. You see, we're operating against massive push forces. We've seen a decade of civil wars erupting in one of the most unstable regions on the planet

---

* Some call this a conscience but I'm fairly certain it's indigestion.

† I'll add it to the list that includes economic reports and showering.

and a crisis spread around the world as millions attempt to flee. If we don't deter these people from fleeing our way, your otherwise perfectly lovely island home—which relies on tourism for about six per cent of its GDP—will soon be overrun with people selfishly seeking sanctuary for their families. It is thereby incumbent on all of us to make coming to Australia seem as hideous and cruel as staying in an area being bombed daily by multiple aggressors.

It's a theory that I first came across when my neighbours' home caught alight. Much to my chagrin I saw the fleeing family look towards my beautiful home as a possible refuge. Thinking quickly, I set my house ablaze too and learned a valuable lesson: if you destroy everything that makes you helpful to someone, you won't be obliged to help them.

Thus began my pioneering campaign to save Australia from these terrifying people eager to share in our way of life. Back in the 1980s it was easy; you just put Paul Hogan in a TV commercial. Since then we've had to move on to more exotic measures.

Thankfully, since the general public know so little about our human rights obligations and the people-smuggling industry, we can easily claim whatever has just been exposed is necessary. People smugglers exploit refugees out of greed, whereas we exploit refugees out of the goodness of our hearts. If anything, crushing a child's will is a charitable act. Anyone who sees the haunted, empty look in the child's eyes will know not to risk fleeing oppression and tyranny when all that awaits is more oppression and tyranny.

Of course, this has become harder since the Papua New Guinea government ruled that our offshore detention system hurt the feelings of its weak and overly-sensitive Constitution. The Australian government has been under pressure to find new locations for our hellish detention facilities. Basically, what we need is a self-storage system for people. We're looking to chuck them in a shed somewhere with the intention of coming back in a few months to pick out the worthwhile stuff—but really, we'll just leave it there and try our best to forget about it.

To this end, I've taken the liberty of ranking the locations currently proposed for offshore detention so that I may give my personal evaluation:

1 *Cambodia*: Sounds weird, awful and far away. Five stars.

2 *New Zealand*: This location would work as part of a long-term psychological attack. It relies on absolute commitment from all participants towards the singular goal of convincing all resettled refugees that they are in Australia. The detainees will slowly be driven mad by the absurdity of the left-wing utopia and beg to be taken back into the sweet authoritarian order of their prison.

3 *Malaysia*: The major strike against this option is that Labor thought it was a good idea so obviously it must be a terrible one. I have done no further research on the matter.

4 *The United States*: This was a late entrant and I'll admit I was initially sceptical. The United States has always been a little too soft on immigrants for my liking, ever since the French accidentally left a giant woman in New York and the locals felt obliged to follow her bidding lest she re-animate and crush them all to smithereens. Recently, however, we've been seeing behaviour from the United States that would absolutely shock the modern Australian to their core, had they not also been tacitly accepting the same kind of stuff for the better part of a decade. It said a lot about our country that when the rest of the world was appalled by Trump's Muslim ban, Turnbull was first on the phone to make sure our refugee resettlement deal still went through. That's commitment beyond distraction.

The bleeding hearts may call us cruel, Orwellian and needlessly sadistic but what we truly are is concerned. Apparently in this modern politically correct culture you are not allowed to voice certain concerns. According to these reality-fearing Leftists, it's now racist to have preconceptions about people based entirely on their race.

Now, before I go on, I feel it's important, lest I be dragged before the Human Rights Commission again, to say that I am not intending to be racist here. I had an epiphany the other week: I realised that Islam is not technically a race. Sure, perhaps I'm hinting towards particular regions with Islam as a dominate religion so as to make it racially charged conversation—but just because I'm not particularly interested in also discussing say, Indonesia, with the world's largest Muslim population and a peaceful ally of Australia for decades, it doesn't make me racist. In fact, if you pay attention, I'm actually attacking these people on the basis of their religion. I'm not racist, I'm merely persecuting a minority for their faith.

Anyway, my concerns aren't for myself. No, not at all. I'm much too evolved for that. This is no silly panic attack or fear of the Other. Rather, I am fundamentally concerned about the freedom of women. I'm passionate about defending the rights of women against the looming spectre of sharia law. And just because my sudden panic doesn't track with my opposition to all other women's rights, such as safe access to abortions, domestic violence, leave and any kind of representation in business or media, doesn't mean my interest isn't valid. Everybody has to start somewhere and I've chosen this issue to make a stand.

This is why I will not relent on my campaign to ban the burqa, the niqab and the full-face cricket helmet. It is my belief that Muslim women should not be forced by a repressive religion to wear any of these garments but rather be forced by a repressive government to not wear any of these garments. That's what freedom looks like.

It's not simply a personal preference. I'm concerned about security. This clothing hides the identity of the wearer and could be used to commit crimes. Now, I realise at this point there isn't any evidence of this being a widespread problem but that's probably because the evidence is all hidden under a niqab. We simply cannot allow the covering of the face in this manner. It is not safe for the rest of us. It's the same reason we banned goatees, sunglasses, face paint, baseball caps and handkerchiefs.

By now, I'm used to howls from my opposition that this is a dog-whistle and a deeply disproportionate response considering how few people in this nation actually wear full or even partial face coverings, but to that I ask, can we be sure of the actual number? Perhaps there are thousands of people under that handful of burqas. We just don't know. This is why my work is so important and necessary.

The fact of the matter is this isn't a numbers issue for me. As long as there is one woman wearing a garment that I have presumed she doesn't wish to wear then I will interfere with her life to make sure she cannot wear it. Frankly, I'm setting people free whether or not they want to be free or even considered themselves to be imprisoned in the first place.

And if this truly is a race issue, then explain my years of pulling off nuns' habits just to make sure they're not hiding anything.

We must halt the spread of sharia law wherever we can see it encroaching. Even if we cannot see it encroaching at all we need to ardently work to ensure it cannot start to encroach. The general public have been too coddled to realise how close we are to the brink of destruction. While there aren't currently any serious advocates for sharia law in Australia, all they would need is one powerful voice. That powerful voice would then need to win an overwhelming majority of seats in both the lower and upper house and then institute sweeping changes to the nation's laws, including quite a few referendums, just to get all these various measures passed—but once they'd done that instituting sharia law would be a breeze.

This is why I consider it incredibly important that parties such as One Nation have a specific policy regarding Islam. I've read the policy and I'd like to take a moment to highlight just what an important piece of writing it is. It'd be the modern Sermon on the Mount if the

Sermon on the Mount was about how immigrants are weird and gross. The policy opens strongly, declaring 'Australia is a country built on Christian values,' which is important to say even if it's not technically true. The subject then nimbly turns to establishing that Australia follows a secular constitution. Again, this is a vitally important point. These religious groups need to know that Australia is a secular *and* Christian nation. We do not have a set religion but if we did it would be Christian and it would be great. That's intrinsic to the Australian experience.

The policy document doesn't simply waste time with lofty proclamations. It also aims to educate the general public about Islam. Even proponents of Islam would do well to read this text as there's a great deal I suspect even they don't know. One good example is that believers of Islam do not support democracy. That's shocking and would come as a surprise to the average Australian, not to mention anyone from Indonesia, Malaysia, Bangladesh, Pakistan, Egypt, Morocco, Tunisia or Algeria, amongst others.

This must be because One Nation is the only party openly speaking about these issues. Everyone else is too cowardly to publish such things without confirmation. Who else would dare to publish such an incontrovertible fact as this:

> It has been noted throughout the world that as long as the Muslim
> population remains around or under 2 per cent in any given country,
> they will be for the most part, regarded as 'a peace-loving minority
> and not a threat to other citizens'.

The nation doesn't matter, the socio-economic and political factors don't matter. The simple fact is, as soon as three in every hundred people practise Islam the entire society is under threat.

Now, two per cent may seem like an absurdly low number to you, but you have to realise that we are talking about over half of half of half of half of half of half of the entire population. It's an epidemic. No wonder we're being swamped!

People are afraid to discuss the population size when it comes to immigration but I have no such fear. A very interesting thesis I read on the bumper sticker of a Toyota Hilux the other day posited the prospect that Australia is full, and I have to say I agree. This whole place has felt a little cramped to me since 1975, to be honest. That was the last time I can remember really being able to stretch my legs.

The statistics prove it. Over the last decade Australia's population has skyrocketed to over two and a half people per square kilometre. This is a shocking figure, particularly considering that if all two and a half are Muslim the entire society is under threat. By comparison, Vatican City currently has four and a half popes per square kilometre and I would hate to see Australia as overrun with people as the Vatican is infested with popes.

But the brilliance of the One Nation party is realising that the terrifying effects of encroaching sharia law isn't simply a numbers game.

It has a stated policy on Islam which unflinchingly addresses all the ways in which sharia law is influencing our society, beginning with identifying a series of horribly un-Australian developments occurring right now:

> Christmas carols can no longer be sung at some schools, bibles will not be found in most hospitals, some public swimming baths have time set aside for Muslim women only, and driver's licences obtained by Muslim women allow them to wear the burqa or niqab. Prayer rooms are now provided in universities, hospitals, schools, airports and shopping centres to accommodate Muslims; this includes Islamic prayer rooms in Christian schools.

Needless to say, each of these is disgusting in its own unique way. While I do not have evidence that children are being physically beaten, if not killed, for singing 'Rudolph the Red-nosed Reindeer' in a public school, I would say that if it is occurring it should be condemned. That I can imagine such an event occurring is sickening to me and it's unconscionable that the media are ignoring it until it actually happens. That bibles cannot be found in most hospitals is even more shocking. To think that hospitals now employ armed guards who confiscate your bible at the door and flush it down the toilet is just unimaginable.

The rest of these complaints show just how low we have sunk already. I'm offended to my core to discover that Muslim women are given time to enjoy a public pool in the town where they live simply because their taxes also help pay for the pool. What am I supposed to do? Swim another time? This is unacceptable. There's only one time of day I want to swim and it's whenever this Muslim pool party is happening.

And don't get me started on prayer rooms. It's horrifying to know that buildings in our society contain rooms that are ostensibly exactly the same as every other room except people are technically allowed to pray in them. For my money, this confirms my right to kick down any locked door I see just in case there are Muslims hiding behind it.

Fortunately, One Nation is not simply wallowing in the problems like other Australian political parties. It's being proactive, with the following series of solutions:

1   *Call for an inquiry or Royal Commission to determine if Islam is a religion or political ideology.* Now, you know me. I believe most government inquiries are really brought together to answer the question of how to most efficiently waste my taxpayer dollars but in this case I'll make an exception. It's imperative we know if Islam is a religion or a political ideology for two reasons: firstly, a great number of people follow this religion and they deserve to know if their devotion is actually just political activism and, secondly, if it is, we're wasting those prayer rooms!

2 *Stop further Muslim immigration and the intake of Muslim refugees until we can assure the safety of Australians.* I do not understand how this notion could even be considered controversial. They're not saying that genuine refugees are a threat. They're just saying we need to keep them out until we can be certain of our own safety. And that's not to say that immigration is directly affecting our safety.* Just that we need things sorted out here first: let's get the road toll down to zero, and decrease heart disease rates, and all those other things, then we can worry about immigration.

3 *Ban the burqa and niqab in public places.* This is the real focal point of the One Nation campaign and a policy it has been proudly flaunting. And why not? This is about the Australian way of life! Australians would never support someone in a full face covering unless they were also holding a cricket bat or the covering was made out of metal and they only wore it when killing police officers. Beyond that, it's a security issue! Who knows what they could be doing under there? Trying to live their lives in privacy? Unacceptable! We're trying to protect the freedoms of our nation and the only way to do that is to violate someone's right to privacy and freedom of religion. Only by openly humiliating and victimising Australian citizens and compromising everything we believe in will we truly ensure our nation remains great.

Yet still people oppose these measures and try to appeal to the weak emotions of those who can still feel, demanding we completely open our borders to people who have already been through various security checks. It's simply unsafe.

The Left, knowing they've lost the battle with reasonable adults, have taken to trying to get children onside to ensure a polling advantage in a decade or so. The Safe Schools program is only the beginning of

---

* Though, of course, we will need to update our percentages to know that.

the brainwashing in our schools. Just last year we heard reports of children as young as nine being taught about the children in detention who are as young as nine. One of the greatest failures of children is their inability to separate logic from emotion. They will hear about these stories of children just like them being kept in what is essentially a prison, despite having committed no crime, and they will cry their little eyes out and demand the children be set free. This is typical of the emotional behaviour of children.

What these children are incapable of realising is that it's actually a good strategy to have children in detention. If we want to be taken seriously about border protection we cannot yield even slightly. When we lock innocent children in offshore detention, people around the world know we mean business, that we're capable of anything. By putting our borders ahead of our own morality we are able to protect our nation from being overrun by hordes of needy children.

My detractors have tried to say I contradict myself on this issue but personally, I think my stance is perfectly clear:

1 Having children in detention is morally permissible.
2 Having children learning about children in detention is disgusting.

The only argument against offshore detention that holds any weight for me is the inordinate cost: $400,000 per year per person! I had assumed that, having cut every possible corner on conditions, we would be making a figurative killing on this accommodation, and not just the occasional literal one. Honestly, for a quarter of that money we could put these refugees up in the Hilton for a year. Or better yet, we could pop them in prison and put me in the Hilton for a year.

Still, I catch myself sometimes wondering what else we could be doing with that taxpayer money. And the answer comes back to me: I would just be spending it on imprisoning refugees anyway. There are some things more important than money and enabling ongoing cruelty is one of them. Ours is a truly great nation and so it takes a lot of effort to make it truly unappealing to everyone overseas. That's why we need to invest in these detention centres, to secure damning United Nations reports and help discourage visitors. You can't put a price on that publicity.

Anyway, if we're short of money we can just take it out of welfare.

8 | How I Solved Race Relations by Ignoring Them

'Who is more racist? The racist, or the person who notices the racism thus confirming its existence?'

—PETER CHUDD, PHILOSOPHICALLY

These days I check my privilege as often as I check my prostate. The result is always the same: it's engorged, incredibly sensitive and best ignored.

My adversaries love to harp on about the advantages I've had in life, as if they couldn't have gone to a private college in a private school on a private island.* The simple fact of the matter is that my dominance in the media can come from only one of two options:

1   I am the most talented, thoughtful and brilliant person to ever walk the Earth and as such it is only natural that every media organisation in the nation would be salivating to get my thoughts on every single program, or

2   I have somehow benefited from privilege in my life.

Obviously, only one of these options is in any way likely.

---

*   The fact of the matter is they couldn't have—but that's because we need to keep it private!

When you talk to the people in the media you will quickly realise that while Australian broadcasters are overwhelmingly white and male they have also all been chosen on their merit. It's a remarkable coincidence—a marvel of statistics akin to winning a lottery—that just so happens to occur in almost every industry around the world.

It's outrageous that people believe I have achieved so much purely because I had an unfair advantage. It's naked jealousy! They wish they had what I had. It's true, they don't even deny it: they openly wish they had the same benefits I have had.

Even so, my success is all my own. Anyone who knows me knows I pulled myself up by the golden bootstraps my father gifted me upon my first steps. Not only that, my success helps others. It's inspirational. People must see me sitting on panels at major festivals or being interviewed on television and think to themselves, 'If he can do it, anyone can!'

The most galling part is how my foes consistently attack me purely on the basis that I'm accidentally white! I do not consider my cultural background so much a privilege as a burden. Honestly, you can see the expectations placed on me just by checking our television guide: anyone from another background or identification would only be expected to speak to their special interest group but I am forced to appear on every show and run opposition to all of them. As a representative of the majority I am greatly outnumbered.

I didn't choose to be part of the dominant culture—I just benefited from it my whole life. Sometimes I like to think of myself as a *Real Housewife of Western Dominance*. I've become accustomed to a certain level of cultural whitewashing and will need to have that maintained.

It's fortunate for everyone else that I can rise above such pettiness myself. I would never notice someone's race, gender or hairstyle. I try to treat everyone as if they're a default human: white and male. That's the core problem of our society—we're constantly noticing things about each other and deciding to discuss them instead of just staying quiet and letting everything keep trucking along.

I am beyond race. I'm so enlightened I don't notice, experience or engage in issues of race. I have long said that race doesn't matter . . . unless we're discussing crime reporting. That's one instance where it's irresponsible to not focus exclusively on someone's cultural background.*

I'm what is called 'post-racial', a term afforded to people who are so thoughtfully beyond primitive notions of race that they have trouble even conceiving of its importance to other people. For this, I'm labelled privileged. Well, let me tell you: it is a privilege, but also a duty.

This was a conscious choice. For too long my work was halted by constant, baseless accusations of racism when I had already carefully examined my own statements and concluded they weren't racist at all. My motivations were never hateful or degrading, but positive. If my accusers could peek into my heart for just a moment they would see this. Sadly, they can only judge me on my words and actions. My attackers claim that I shouldn't talk about racism since I don't experience it—but isn't that the worst kind of racism? To assume that I don't experience racism purely on the basis of my race?

To be sure, the scientific establishment might criticise me for my breakthrough in finding and categorising the rumoured 'crime gland' but it's not surprising that people with their skull shape are judgemental of phrenology; they have the ridges of the intolerant and the indents of the childish.

I wish for a tolerant society, so I choose to be of a neutral race. But others seem compelled to take their race with them wherever they go! They never just leave it at the door so as to not make the rest of us uncomfortable. It's selfish, really.

---

*   Provided it's not default white, in which case there were probably other factors.

I do not believe that my whiteness matters. If anything, this is the defining tenet of whiteness. White culture is all about living in a society so advantageous to you that notions of the construct of race never really enter your mind, aside from a passing interest in why people are so upset at the Oscars every year.

To not care about race is truly one of the greatest cultural benefits of being white—and other races compelling me to recognise this, acknowledge this and then stop actively hurting them, infringes on my cultural freedom. People like to claim that white people have no culture but that's absurd. Just as white is a mix of all colours, so too white culture is a pick-and-choose assortment of all the things we've enjoyed from other cultures and wish to make our own.

This is just one reason why I have such a problem with the concept of cultural appropriation. Take the example of the Native American headdress. I understand that it is a sacred symbol. I recognise that this is a culture where its very survival until this point is remarkable and therefore these signifiers become incredibly powerful and representative to members of that culture. I understand the pain and trauma that is associated with these artefacts. I have just decided to disregard it.

Equally, can they not see my innate right to not feel bad about trampling on another culture's heritage because I think it is a funny hat? All I am asking is that we respect each other's opinions here. We hear so much about tolerance, but it's telling just how intolerant the Left can be when it comes to my choice to disregard tolerance. If there were justice in the world the Leftists would be consistent to what I imagine their standpoint to be, and preach nothing but passive tolerance as I slowly beat them.

As you can see, I have been forced to become post-racial as a matter of self-preservation; it affords me plausible deniability from any race-related issues and also my own sense of social responsibility. Still, I will endeavour to give my commentary on all race relations—it is my burden as a white man*—but I promise you, I am not doing this to further the wedge between the races, but rather so that the differences can finally be ignored and my ultimate goal of bringing about racial harmony will have been achieved.

I'll give you an example of how it works. Am I Indigenous? Technically, no. But even more technically: yes! This is a fun thing I do. I claim that I am 'indigenous', in the sense that I was born in the nation in which I'm currently residing. This clever use of a homonym allows me to attempt to erase the identity of Aboriginal people. You see, all it takes is for someone to call themselves Indigenous in a wilful misinterpretation of what the words are intended to signify! Do not get me wrong, I am not trying to claim any form of First Nations identity. I'm perfectly happy being as white as the driven snow. I think being white is supremely good. I'm merely trying to show that other people's identity really means nothing to me and can be taken away by a simple trick of grammar.

And before you write in—no, I am not aware of any historic parallels to this kind of practice. Assimilation, to my knowledge, has only been tried before in _Star Trek_ episodes and it always seems to work out there. And by wilfully choosing not to do any due diligence on the matter I can remain blissfully ignorant, and it can be as if the events never occurred. Some people will argue that failing to acknowledge this dark history is in itself absolutely disgusting but I have found that it's very difficult to hear those arguments when I have my fingers in my ears.

This is why I find it so strange when people call me ignorant as an insult. My ignorance is a gift! It's a Schrödinger-esque mindset: if I remain entirely ill-informed about history or current social conditions it is impossible to say for sure whether or not they truly exist!

---

*   Formerly, at least, before my enlightenment.

We're constantly being told of the need to 'Close the gap' yet no one is listening to my suggestion to close it by just ignoring it. A gap can only exist between two objects. By refusing to see any difference between the two, I can make the gap itself disappear.

Yet, the Left refuses to acknowledge my scientific discovery. Even the Sydney Trains network attacked me for placing my Don't Mind the Gap posters at local stations.

It's a terrible tragedy that we see these divisions refusing to close. And it's no surprise that once again, I am thrashed with my own olive branch. They tell me that I've stolen the land I'm living on, yet I am able to produce documentation clearly showing that I bought my plot of land fair and square after three years of tireless campaigning to have the housing commission block originally located here sold off and demolished.

It's not as if I have personally stolen anything! Even if you accept that the land was stolen, that was a long time ago. So what if I'm still in possession of the land? It's not as if there are any laws against holding on to stolen property long after it was originally taken. Telling me to go back to where I came from is a nasty slur that should be reserved for refugees fleeing tyranny.

I'm doing my duty. I have a responsibility to dilute everyone else's identity as quickly as possible, so that they too may know the pleasure of being a white man in the modern world. We hear that the life of the white male is so privileged and blessed and yet when I try to share this good fortune* I'm lambasted! Surely, it's a generous and kind act to treat everyone as if they had the same privilege as me, so that in time they too may come to believe it. This is why I'm adamant I'll climb Uluru the second my knee, ankle and lower back heal and my

---

*   Metaphorically, of course. No one is getting their hands on my precious money.

respiratory issues are fully resolved. Sure, from the outset it would seem to be a shocking act of wilful disrespect but, again, I'm trying to show a respect that goes beyond the acknowledgement of someone's wishes.

Besides, it's a matter of principle! In a supposedly free world, how can restrictions be placed on my movements? It's like living under the heel of a totalitarian dictatorship. Sure, there aren't any laws preventing you from climbing the large rock and people still do it every day, but without a guarantee that I will be able to complete the full journey without any form of judgement then I might as well be in a Russian gulag, as far as I'm concerned. And frankly, that it's become somehow offensive to climb on the rock just because it's sacred is an outrageous double standard! Not once have I ever stopped an Indigenous person from attempting to climb on my church just to have a look around. Of course, if anyone tried I would be shocked and outraged but then that would be an entirely different situation in which I was the aggrieved party. That would be untenable.

At this juncture, I must admit that despite my best efforts, I have been the victim of racism—in fact, even worse: reverse racism. For the uninformed amongst my readers, I admire your dedication to ignorance, but in this case I urge you to pay attention as this affects me. Reverse racism is like racism but without any of the structural power that comes with it—which makes it even worse, as I'm completely unprepared for attack! Unfortunately, reverse racism has become all too familiar in modern Australia. I'm sorry to say it has even been endorsed by the government through the dreadful Human Rights Commission. Just think: a racist idea being promoted by the Australian government!

The Human Rights Commission are obsessed with human rights to the point of mania. It's pathetic, really. It's as if human rights violations are the only thing they're capable of talking about. Not only are they always talking about these violations, they're always complaining! They hardly ever celebrate a right really well violated—there's no appreciation for the craftsmanship of the oppressor anymore. They have now whipped themselves into such a frenzy that they jump and shriek even at the slightest run-of-the-mill degradation of someone's spirit.

To make matters worse, the group is clearly terribly biased, stacked with people resolutely opposed to human rights violations. It's a complete lack of balance that shreds the credibility of the institution. For true objectivity, the panel would need to be half the current lot and half people willing to consider that sometimes violation of human rights can be a necessary evil. What is the point of a Human Rights Commission incapable of deciding whether a human rights violation was for the greater good? From a philosophical standpoint, it's reminiscent of collectors who keep their action figures in the original packaging and never get them out to play.

The influence of politically correct culture is again evidenced by the sensitivity shown even for the people within the Human Rights Commission. As my contemporary Tim Blair noted, [Race Discrimination Commissioner] Tim Soutphommasane's name would 'be a 23-point certainty for the board game hall of fame if only Scrabble allowed proper nouns'. The Left went wild, claiming it was 'offensive' or 'not a particularly good joke, just pretty cheap and sad'. But really, this is a brilliant satire based on how Mr Blair finds Mr Soutphommasane's name weird and also it's quite a bit longer than his own name. If Soutphommasane didn't want to be the butt of jokes like this he should have had a normal last name, like Blair. If this joke had any fault, it was just that the name is more than seven letters so wouldn't work in Scrabble. Also, it accidentally reveals that my friend Tim believes a 23-point word in Scrabble would be worthy of a hall of fame, which suggests he's just really very bad at Scrabble in a variety of ways. But otherwise, this joke is perfect.

Still, it gets to the heart of the matter. The idea that Australia could be racist is so absurd it could have only been thought up by the weirdest foreigner as a part of one of their strange and hilarious customs. We're the nation that repealed the White Australia policy, after we were asked to stop being so explicitly racist in our immigration laws. A few years later we even stopped trying to enact the White Australia policy by proxy. We've also gone almost fifteen years without a full race riot. Sure, you get a little smattering of a race 'rally' that isn't exactly harmonious but they rarely completely riot.

We are a multicultural nirvana.* It is a shame that the serenity of our post-racial paradise is so often tarnished by people complaining they've been racially vilified. I am not trying to claim racism doesn't exist. Of course racism exists in other nations. It's simply that Australia solved racism the day we generously gave Waleed Aly the Gold Logie for best nailing of it, whatever the 'it' may be. That squared the ledger. Now that we gave that one person that one award I think it's time everyone else calmed down and just got on with it. Heck, it could even count as reparations for all the land stolen over the years by Scotty Cam while making The Block.

But unfortunately, the outrage brigade has overruled me again. Nowhere is this more evident than in the discussion of the unjust 18C laws. Those trying to silence me argue I am compromised on this issue. They believe that the fact that I was the first, and so far only, person in Australian history to be tried, found guilty, and then publicly tarred and feathered by Governor-General Peter Cosgrove during an Australia Day ceremony means that I am not in a position to comment on the validity of these laws. In fact I am the perfect person to discuss this issue because I have been through the system and come out the other side. The Chookening has only strengthened my resolve.

---

* And no, I am not referring to the 'politically correct' reimagining of the Seattle grunge band which replaced Dave Grohl with a woman of colour.

Make no mistake, the battle over Section 18C is the frontline of free speech in our nation. While from the outside it might seem more pressing to enact laws to prevent whistleblowers from exposing abuse in our detention centres, this is not the case and I can explain why. As far as I understand it, the *Border Force Act* is finally being used to quiet the constant complaints about detention centre conditions from bleeding heart doctors and medical professionals. That these people have been shut up isn't an injustice, it's a miracle! Yes, of course, it is less than ideal that there are laws banning speech but we have to ask ourselves whether we'd really want these people talking anyway. We've copped a break that some people are traumatised beyond speaking and others have sewed their mouths closed in a desperate plea for help, but we will not always be this lucky.

Even if we did fight to have the *Border Force Act* overturned we'd just be doing it to hear a whole lot more whingeing about conditions and hardly anything from all the people who love being in indefinite detention.* That isn't my idea of 'valued speech', so it isn't worth defending.

What *is* worth defending is my right to say whatever I like in my column without suffering the indignity of criticism.

It's undeniable that silencing me will have a much greater effect than silencing your average citizen. From the perspective of sheer airtime, I'm on multiple platforms during prime time at least five days a week, whereas refugees hardly ever appear, even on Sunday morning political shows.

That's why I'm so focused on repealing the risible Section 18C of the laughable *Racial Discrimination Act* which, despite its name, has not once

---

* They do exist and you cannot prove they don't, particularly as it's almost impossible to get any communication from people inside these centres.

helped me racially discriminate against anyone. I've included the law below, which, in my opinion, is worse than any possible racial slur*:

Offensive behaviour because of race, colour or national or ethnic origin

(1) It is unlawful for a person to do an act, otherwise than in private, if:

    (a) the act is reasonably likely, in all the circumstances, to offend, insult, humiliate or intimidate another person or a group of people; and

    (b) the act is done because of the race, colour or national or ethnic origin of the other person or of some or all of the people in the group.

Now, this is a complicated bit of legalese so I'll walk you through it. On face value, what this law claims is that if I want to offend, insult, humiliate or intimidate another person or group of people on the basis of their race I will have to do so in private.

This is incredibly burdensome. When the law was first enacted I tried to keep up but found myself needing to duck into a telephone booth every time I wanted to express myself, like a deeply problematic Superman. It was during these moments, hunched over and whispering ethnic slurs to myself inside a telephone booth, that I realised something had to be done about this law.

It's time we admitted that 18C is dangerous. The constant threat of being called racist puts undue stress on people's lives, unlike racial vilification, which has never hurt anyone.

Legal experts recognise that there is a significant problem with the use of the words 'insult' and 'offend' in this law. I agree. For starters,

---

*   My editors insisted I remove my complete and unabridged list.

these jokers are acting like insulting and offending people is terrible when it's actually just a bit of good old-fashioned Australian banter. Senator David Leyonhjelm brilliantly exposed the pointlessness of Section 18C by complaining to the Human Rights Commission about being called an angry white male. The biased media mocked him and claimed it was pathetic, transparent and incredibly petty but I knew better: it was a brilliant piece of performance art. By deliberately misusing the system, the good senator proved it was possible for the system to be deliberately misused. We now know that if these laws are not used in the manner in which they were intended, they could actually be harmful.*

How revolting to say that these laws weren't intended for the use of white men. Why should anything be made if it is not intended to be used by white men? It's raw discrimination. We have to remember that when you punish the white male you are punishing the default human. This means everyone suffers. Especially white men. Eventually, the cowards at the Human Rights Commission rejected the senator's complaint on the grounds that he wasn't truly offended by the comments, which is ridiculous. Once again, Leyonhjelm was punished for having thick white skin.

Some have argued that this swift rejection of his claim was proof that frivolous complaints don't pass muster but actually it's just proof that this anti-discrimination group is actually a cabal dedicated to discrimination against white men. Leyonhjelm brilliantly exposed this law for exactly what it is: the Anti-White Australia Policy.†

---

* It's the same point I proved to my beautiful and powerful son Rand when I drank all the liquids I found under the sink. Although the week I spent in a coma caused me great personal harm and a large financial loss, it beautifully demonstrated my argument.

† This is a clever play on a brilliant but forgotten racist policy we once had before political correctness ruined everything.

The political correctness police say there's no such thing as racism against white people but they said the same thing about the Sasquatch and I've seen him with my own eyes. They say that racism is another form of structural oppression and that you cannot be 'racist' towards a group with all the power and opportunity, but the truth is you can and that's why it hurts even more. We've been softened by years of privilege. Attacking us is like pressing on a baby's fontanelle. Racism against white people is also shocking because it's so unusual. We're used to all other racism by now—it's completely normal—but this? It still chills me.

The way racism against white people manifests is disgusting too, such as labelling me—one of the last good and pure people on this planet—with horrific slurs such as 'racist'. Do people not understand that being called a racist is the most hurtful thing you could possibly say to me? These feeble-minded people don't understand that this word prejudges me and indicates a lack of respect for my innate humanity. I cannot currently think of any other examples of such a thing but that's probably because nothing compares to the pain I feel every day.

It's particularly incredulous because any media monitor worth their salt knows that when you truly examine any news story, it's the person calling someone else racist who ends up being the true racist. It's an academic truism that I describe as the 'whomever smelt it most likely dealt it' principle.

Honestly, look at the media cycle of any controversial news story on the issue of race in our recent history and it will follow the same pattern.

Day One

The story breaks. People open their office windows to scream in rage at the heavens for daring to allow such a travesty to occur.

Day Two

The outrage continues simply because the perpetrator refuses to apologise. The backlash to the backlash begins, lasting at least an hour before the backlash to the backlash to the backlash beats on like petulant waves striking the shore.

Day Three

An insightful columnist (most likely yours truly) realises that the real victim is actually the perpetrator. Everyone is shocked at the undeniable logic. They meekly apologise to me, lower their heads in defeat and solemnly march back into the Centrelink office.

It happens this way every time and yet no one ever learns.

Nowadays, the second a controversy erupts I look to see who is being accused of wrongdoing and jump to their defence before bothering to get the nitty-gritty details. It saves time and eventually I'll be proven right anyway so I think of it as getting in on a band before they're cool.

So, I battle on. Frankly, it's amazing that I have the strength to help others at all considering what I go through every day. I don't do it for the accolades, though yes, I do deserve them. I do it because I must. I do it because I can't let the other side win.

In truth, no one knows my suffering. I am without a doubt the most abused person on the internet. If you were merely tracking the volume of hateful comments sent my way you would have to assume I was some combination of female Ghostbuster who shot a beloved gorilla before jumping on a plane to Africa.

Yet, I am an adult: I can choose not to be offended. Of course, I am yet to exercise this choice as it greatly helps my business to be constantly riled up online, but the fact remains that I have that option.

Why can't everyone realise they have this? The next time you are being horribly abused on the bus, why don't you decide that you aren't going to be abused anymore? Problem solved. It's all about your state of mind. Reality is what you make it.

In fact, racism can only exist if you allow it to exist. By simply refusing to acknowledge it, it will go the way of the old gods and drift into non-existence. People call me a monster for refusing to acknowledge clear and present racism but truly I am performing a greater service.

Of course, part of the Human Rights Commission's devilish game is that it's difficult to discuss precisely why I need these laws to be repealed without violating them. But we in the media have long since developed a trick for this exact situation. What we do is vaguely reference needing to have an 'honest' discussion. Honest, in this case, is code for 'deeply racist but without consequences'. In calling for an honest discussion you get to imply that there's a terrific point that you would love to make but you simply can't on account of it being considered deeply offensive.

For the record, that is exactly the situation I am in right now. The second this law is repealed I will be able to make the terrific point I have been trying to make all along. Legally, I am not able to tell you exactly what it is, but trust me, it's a doozy. I've tried to explain myself without violating the law but it's just impossible. That's how tightly bound these restrictions have made us.

Even the supposed protections do not work. Just take a look at Section 18D:

Exemptions
Section 18C does not render unlawful anything said or done reasonably and in good faith:
(a) in the performance, exhibition or distribution of an artistic work; or

(b) in the course of any statement, publication, discussion or debate made or held for any genuine academic, artistic or scientific purpose or any other genuine purpose in the public interest; or

(c) in making or publishing:

(i) a fair and accurate report of any event or matter of public interest; or

(ii) a fair comment on any event or matter of public interest if the comment is an expression of a genuine belief held by the person making the comment.

Now, let's cut through this boffin-speak to see how these protections do not apply to me.

First, my column is not an artistic work as it has a purpose and doesn't waste taxpayer money. Furthermore, while my work on this matter technically does draw on a kind of science, it is not considered scientific enough anymore by the ruling establishment to class it as an academic text. Fortunately, everything I do is in the public interest, but with that brief clemency comes another wave of tyranny: I'm confined to only reporting events or matters in a 'fair and accurate' way or through an 'expression of a genuine belief'. This leaves little room to lie or exaggerate to serve a specific purpose. If that simply ended with the majority of satirists being thrown in prison then I'd be perfectly happy, but as it is it just cripples my business model.

The fact of the matter is someone is always going to be 'offended' by your work. This is particularly true if your entire business model is based on people clicking on your column to see what horribly offensive thing you've said today.

Yet more and more we see waves of this 'outrage' at absolutely everything. Personally, I find it outrageous. There's nothing that makes me more furious than to see people getting mad for no reason. And sure, you will hear the usual crowd bleating how strange it is for an advocate of unrestricted free speech to complain when people exercise that freedom to criticise him, but actually it makes perfect sense.

As I've said before, all criticism is censorship. At no moment was this more clear than when I came under attack for a harmless satirical speech I gave pillorying some of the more amusing races I have noticed for customs which are clearly and objectively weird and yucky.

As always, the humourless Left missed the joke and cried 'racism'. Luckily, you and I know that's just a word they like to use when something is too accurate in its sweeping generalisation of another race.

It was not the first nor the last time I've received such hysteria. My previous speech 'Reasons Why ISIS Is Actually Very Good' was a hilarious romp, if I may say so myself, subversively detailing how the Islamic State occasionally ruthlessly murders people that I already don't like. A net positive for me!

The detractors, with their pitchforks and flaming torches, seemed completely incapable of understanding that this was all just a joke. That's right—a joke! People like to think that because an artist claims their work to be trenchant satire it's attempting to make a point beyond comedy but this is not true. When something is a joke it demands no analysis beyond the subjective measure of whether or not it's funny. Anything beyond this would give a satirist the inflated idea that their artistic work is an attempt to effect social change, whereas in fact satirists just fart-arse around collecting paycheques and complaining about society, not influencing it.

Seeing all these attempts to understand the point of jokes infuriates me as much as people analysing the brush technique of the Mona Lisa. It's just a painting of a nice lady almost smiling. Who cares about anything else?

Nowhere is this indignant overanalysis worse than in the cesspool of the internet known as Twitter. Every day this pathetic website discharges fresh umbrage from hordes of professionally offended people trying to ruin my day. The most disappointing part is that Twitter once had such promise. When I first joined, I was pleased to discover it seemed to be an ambitious sociological experiment, attempting to collect and categorise all currently known forms of mental illness. Unfortunately, it soon became overrun by the greatest mental illness of all: Leftism.

And of course, my hilarious speech was just another excuse to boil over. The rabid Leftist Twitter warriors tore me to shreds, calling my work 'bad', and also 'not very good at all'. Though, if I had known then what I know now I would have counted my blessings. It seems a short time later that someone decided to send a recording of the speech to the Australian Human Rights Commission. The bleeding hearts naturally salivated at the chance to drag another proud thought-leader over the coals and so they set a bounty for my capture dead or alive.*

Not only is it an utter disgrace that I was dragged in front of the Human Rights Commission, it was a complete waste of time. Heck, I would argue it was exactly the same kind of brutal violence that I was satirising by tacitly endorsing! This is not an absurd comparison. Every complaint to the Human Rights Commission is practically a bullet from the Islamic State, and the brutal force used by these social justice warriors to attempt to keep me quiet was clearly the legal equivalent of the sacking of Palmyra.

Make no mistake, as well: the people who endorse these measures definitely also endorse the work of the Islamic State. There is absolutely no middle ground here. People like to believe there is a gulf between wishing that I would exercise some journalistic integrity and wishing for my execution, but they are one and the same.

---

* Technically, they only specified alive and didn't ask anyone to apprehend me but I believe my point stands.

Just because something isn't graceful, comfortable and aesthetically pleasing doesn't mean it isn't a powerful expression of free speech. I said as much at the Walkleys after shitting myself on stage following a few too many chardonnays. It wasn't an 'accident' as the press so crudely labelled it, but rather a powerful protest against Sarah Ferguson's continued success.

Fortunately, the case was dropped and I was once again allowed to walk free. This earned me my self-appointed title as Australia's Nelson Mandela. The fact that I was never actually imprisoned does nothing to harm this image. It's not my fault my long walk to freedom was more of a gentle stroll.

What is really disappointing is that we wasted valuable time dealing with this garbage that could have been better spent humiliating other lesser people in the first place. The commission should be focusing on much more important work, such as entertaining the petty larks of senators and issuing personal apologies to me.

Still, perhaps the enduring legacy of this whole debacle will be to finally bring to light the fight against Section 18C as the most pertinent battle currently underway in Australia. It is up to us to carry the banner of free speech. We cannot turn our heads and look away; this isn't a humanitarian crisis.

Others will make their excuses. They will say that something is only technically censorship if the person is somehow censored. Perhaps they'll even have the audacity to claim that, even if it's being done for less than desirable reasons, a piece of work being shared further than it would have ever been otherwise is the diametric opposite of censorship.

I am not swayed by such feeble arguments.

I alone have the vision to see that this is all part of the continuing conspiracy to outlaw whiteness. But even I cannot be sure how far the plot spreads, whether to the introduction of sharia law or changes to the terms and conditions of Twitter.

This modern age has seen the implementation of laws designed to supposedly fix racism once and for all by throwing every white person in prison for daring to express an opinion, or commit a hate crime.

What a complete waste of our legal system. We should not be legislating on such petty matters, clogging up the High Court. This is why I have been proposing the reintroduction of trial by combat. It is much simpler and more efficient. Also, since we know that the hand of God will empower the worthy, anyone who refuses a trial by combat is effectively admitting their guilt, even if they're the victim.

But this is just the start. It's time we revolutionised our legal system so it defends the people who need it. We need laws that protect me. I'm the true victim of racism. Not only vile taunts online but more subtle, hurtful racism. Martin Luther King Junior spoke of the soft racism of lowered expectations and I think it's fair to say no one faces lower expectations than I do. I've coined a variant to describe my personal torment: the hard racism of accountability.

You see, thanks to regressive laws like Section 18C, I am no longer able to say what I want without the twin tyrannies of criticism and fact-checking. This is just another way of trying to end my brave fight for what is good and right. I don't think it's going too far to say that the people at the Australian Human Rights Commission, given the chance, would have duct-taped Jesus Christ's mouth shut as he hung on the cross, just in case he whimpered something 'offensive' about the Roman people.

It's important to understand that we're trying to preserve our nation. The entire world is living in fear of terrorists and struggling for answers. At this stage there are only a few things we know for sure: one is that young people who leave Australia to fight in the Middle East are almost always people who believe they do not belong in our society. So what I am trying to do is identify all the people I believe do not belong in Australian society so we can investigate them properly. I'm fairly certain that all we need is a media witch-hunt, followed by extensive and invasive investigation by ASIO, to thoroughly prove that if these young men were not radicalised before they definitely will be now.

Others want to coddle these extremely dangerous radicals, and let them know we have a place for them, but I am concerned this will make them feel as if they're welcome. If there's one thing the last decade has taught us it's that oppressive crackdowns work. We've seen them slowly occurring around the world and personally I have never felt safer.

We're facing enemies unlike anything we've seen before. They are absolute monsters and if defeating them requires that we become worse monsters in almost every demonstrable way, then so be it. Sure, Abraham Lincoln once said 'the fastest way to destroy an enemy is to make them your friend' but he was writing in a time before predator drones. These are even faster.

We need to be able to speak openly about these events, not pay lip-service to political correctness and rely on our audience's ability to infer the racial undertones to our seemingly innocuous dog-whistles.

Luckily, there are some people still willing to stand up for what is right. The Minister for Immigration Peter Dutton was right to note that former Prime Minister Malcolm Fraser made a mistake to increase immigration during his time in office. This was a brave and proud statement by the minister and I applaud him for it. A lesser man would have softened his remarks about the recently deceased prime minister, or at least made the statement while Malcolm Fraser was still alive and able to respond, but he disregarded these niceties because he knew it was the right thing to do.

What Dutton has done—after drawing on my own exceptional research, I'm sure—is finally open the immigration debate to questions not just of an individual's character but also of their hypothetical grandchildren. It's a shame the 'sins of the father' argument has lost its appeal over the years but I've never stopped believing in it. Every infant I see is a reminder of the potential for criminality that exists in human DNA.

Dutton has also made the fine point that many of the people coming into Australia right now cannot read or write. This is so patently true that he didn't bother to support it with evidence, as you'd need to be a fool to not believe it. In my opinion, it's deeply suspicious that someone incapable of reading and writing has even heard of Australia. That's reason for investigation alone. Beyond that, we have to ask, why were these people so desperate to flee their homelands that they couldn't take the time to learn a foreign language?

It used to be that we'd test for exactly these things as part of the White Australia policy, until the political correctness police shut that down. Fortunately, it just became part of the next policy and no one seemed to mind for a while. It was brilliantly effective. You force a potential migrant to sit a literacy exam before entering the country. If they fail, you deny their visa. If they pass, you find another language and test them on that. Repeat this process until they fail.

What I don't understand is how this is an issue at all. If people do not speak the language they should not be entering Australia. This is exactly why the first settlers were so careful to learn and document the languages of all the people they were murdering. It's basic politeness.

If people do not speak English, how am I supposed to eavesdrop on their conversations to make sure they're not plotting anything? My number's been blocked by the Homeland Security Hotline since I reported people for openly speaking Chinese. Besides, how do we expect someone to operate in our nation without learning to speak English? It's not as if any of us will ever even attempt to learn a few phrases in another language to be more accommodating.

These poor people won't even be able to read my columns which argue they should have never been allowed into this country! But then, what's the point in them engaging with our society when I can just tell from their expression that they're secretly plotting to bring an end to our nation?

We simply cannot wait for an attack before deciding to get serious about national security. This is why I have proposed building a large wall around Australia. It seems like a pointless gesture, considering we're an island continent, but if anything, that's what makes it brilliant: let's transform the world's oceans from a welcome mat into our own personal moat.

As we all know, anything that happens in a moat is entirely legal. It's technically counted as international waters, and since Australia excluded itself from its own migration zone there's basically no law at all once you get past the first waves at Bondi.

Obviously I am willing to make exceptions. If someone has experience in an industry in great need then I believe we should do whatever we can to accommodate them. In this case, I am referring to anyone capable of bowling passable finger spin, or perhaps solid leg spin that can tie down one end while the fast bowlers attack on the other side.

I am not claiming we end immigration forever, I'm simply saying that we withdraw for a little while until we achieve the total peace and cohesion we had in the late nineties. It's time for Australia to become the isolated island at the bottom of the world again. We'll just leave an out-of-office note on the Harbour Bridge directing people to New Zealand and take a little bit of 'me' time.

This is a time for choosing. We cannot worry about 'offending' one person or 'falsely accusing' another. We have to stop pretending that racism is a social injustice rather than a useful profiling tool. We have to understand that the cost of liberty is eternal vigilance and the price of freedom is giving up everything that makes you free.

If I can make one promise to you, dear reader, it's this: I will not be silenced. I will not be stopped. And I will not take responsibility for the things I say. That's what freedom of speech is all about.

9

Save the Date: Why we should try our best to forget what happened on Australia Day

'Those who forget the past are doomed to be rewarded with a bloody great time.'
—PETER CHUDD, POWERFULLY

Australia Day is Christmas for patriots.

It's without a doubt the most glorious holiday on the Australian calendar. Sure, it may not have the blockbuster AFL matches of Anzac Day, the blockbuster cricket of Boxing Day or the blockbuster Cake Eating Contest of the Queen's Birthday, but we don't need those. We're too busy celebrating Australia.

At least, that was once the case before the political correctness police tried to destroy Australia Day by changing the date of the celebration in the hope that no one would be able to find it. It seems the holiday is 'offensive' to some! Now the only Australia Day the Left will permit is a vegan soy-sage barbecue chargrilled by burning flags.

Like most Australians, I get my perspective on race relations from meat commercials. It's a wonderful way to understand that, really, we're all united together against vegetarians. That's why I was so pleased to see the 2016 Australia Day campaign from the Meat and Livestock Australia; a spirited follow-up to their previous disappointing commercial which claimed that there weren't enough diverse faces on Australian television—as if the four different expressions I'm capable of pulling aren't diverse enough. The 2017 ad wonderfully flips the outdated 'historically accurate' view of Australia Day on its head and shows that, far from the beginnings of a genocide, the landing of settlers to this land was actually a fun barbecue filled with top celebrities, raucous laughs and selective ignorance. This is the Australia Day that I wish to celebrate. The radical, unstable Left want Australia Day to be a national day of mourning renamed Invasion Day. (They were utterly inflexible when I offered the compromise of Successful British Invasion Celebration Day.)

For a long time now it has been a stated goal of the Left to make loving your country a crime. I'm so guilty of patriotism that if they had their way I'd be thrown in the maximum security prison currently reserved for the most dangerous criminals and youngest asylum seekers.

There have already been rumblings in Western Australia, which I must remind you is Australia's leftmost state geographically. In 2016, Fremantle, the bastard child of Western Australia, attempted to move Australia Day to a date two days later—in what should be considered a cultural coup to overthrow the federal government. When I heard this I vomited right into the burrito bowl I was enjoying. For those who have never been there, it is important to understand that Fremantle is very much the undergraduate arts student of cities. It has no place in a desert and seems to only be there to bum around and find itself. It's in the midst of a hard-work heartland and yet is vacuous, self-obsessed and full of prisons and surf shops. Were Fremantle a person, it would be Scott Ludlam, the Greens Senator from Fremantle, riding a longboard to a yoghurt store. I've come up with a good joke about Fremantle. Here it is: it's surprising they were able to find a day there when everyone was working in order to take a day off!

Let me be very clear: the 26th of January is the greatest and most beautiful day of the year, whereas the 28th is a complete hunk of shit.

Every year, when I buy my calendar, I immediately circle the 26th of January and spit on the 28th before I allow myself to flick through the other months to see which vaccines Mr Leunig has advised me to avoid.

I've heard these calls to 'change the date' and they seem unnecessary because suggesting that Australia Day is tied to the First Fleet's arrival is completely outdated. However—and coincidentally—moving it away from this date would be a disgrace to our ancestors.

In a rare positive move for the public broadcaster, radio lotharios Triple J refused to change the date of their famous Hottest 100 Countdown to accommodate this latest centuries-long protest movement. Perhaps the folks over there were far too busy sniffing their bongs and playing the new stuff from Split Enz to even hear the debate. But credit where credit's due, these layabouts somehow managed to make the right decision. According to the supposed youth broadcaster*, moving the date would be considered 'political'. This is true; to act is political but to ignore something and hope it goes away is apolitical. It puts me in mind of whenever I see a homeless person sleeping rough on the street. Part of me may want to either give them a coin or berate them for being the reason our once-great civilisation is crumbling—but those are both political acts. What I do is to just hold back and wait for winter.

Why then, I must ask, are we still constantly bombarded with calls to change our national day? The answer is simple—and perhaps it is not politically, or even fundamentally, correct but it's important to say all the same: radically Indigenous Australians are trying to prevent us from celebrating Australia Day by reminding us what happened on that day.

---

* I'd suggest they check my ratings breakdown before claiming such a title. Many of my shows are absolutely dominant amongst the youth demographic of 40–55-year-olds.

Australia Day should be a day of fun in the sun, sand and water. It's about having a cold beer by the pool and celebrating being born on the greatest, most problem-free nation on Earth. How could you have a problem with that? In fact, considering the importance the day holds for our gloriously free nation, anyone expressing discontent with it should be thrown straight into prison. At the very least, this would keep up the other great Australian tradition of imprisonment for petty squabbles.

If everyone were just a little more like me, Australia Day would be a beautiful acknowledgement of the freedoms we hold dear. Every year I perform a stirring tribute to our nation in which I lie in a hammock made from an Australian flag and drink an entire case of VB over the course of a morning.

It is incredibly rude to remind someone of genocide when they're trying to have a day off. Why deliberately ruin someone's day by pointing out what they're tacitly celebrating? If I am at a child's birthday party having a cracking time trying to pin the tail on the donkey, it's unseemly to remind me of the Stalinist purges.* The simple fact that the child's birthday party was deliberately scheduled to coincide with the anniversary of these purges is of no relevance, as is whether or not the child is a direct descendant of the purgers still living on the land they purged. All that's important is that I am having a good time and expecting a lolly bag later.

And so all I am asking is that we spend just one day—Australia Day—celebrating being Australian without having to question what it means to be Australian. Why can't we just enjoy being here instead of all this questioning over how we got here? This is just like back in

---

*   Although unfortunately whenever I see people being given lolly bags for nothing
     I am reminded of the horrors of communism.

university when I'd go to a house party and people would be too busy insisting that they hadn't invited me to get on with the partying.

We cannot get bogged down by questions of who massacred whom. We cannot get sidetracked questioning whether we should be celebrating the darkest day in the history of the world's oldest continuing culture. This is part of the reason I always make an effort to be drunk by noon to ensure these creeping thoughts don't haunt me all day.

Too much time is spent obsessing over who is from which culture when really, we're all Australian. Sure, you might have never asked to be Australian, and instead had Australia dropped on top of your home, but all I am saying is to try to make the most of it. Australia Day is not a time for reflection, unless it's the reflection of my large entirely hairless torso as I belly flop into my neighbour's wading pool.

Frankly, you would be hard-pressed to find a day that *doesn't* coincide with a colonising force initiating some form of massacre. While this may prompt some to question whether we should be celebrating at all, I choose to see it as further evidence that changing the date is inherently pointless. You can read historical significance into anything if you want to! Honestly, if you were to really comb over my demands for assimilation on this holiday, there'd probably be some historical parallels with demands by the Australian government that Aboriginal people assimilate as a means of slowly killing off their culture. That doesn't mean it's significant. It just shows that historians are lazy.

Still, there are at least a few dozen virtually massacre-free years to celebrate. Why can't we just enjoy those without worrying about the rest of history? Are we seriously so ashamed of our great nation on account of a little enduring national shame?

It's incredible to me that there are people in Australia who don't love it. Do these people not know that if you do not love a nation you are welcome to leave it? It's as if they haven't read a bumper sticker in their lives. (Let's be very clear before the pernickety Left tries to attack me—if you do not love Australia you are welcome to leave. However, in the case that you do not love, say, Syria and do love Australia, I must insist you stay in Syria.)

It saddens me to say these malcontents have even tainted our beautiful flag.* Protesters have even taken to burning the Australian flag at protests! They should be locked up! Sure, there may technically have been no crime committed since it was their own flag and no total fire ban was in place that day, but it should have been a crime. We need to criminalise burning the flag to preserve the free speech it represents.

It's disgusting to me that the Left would stoop to burning flags! It's as if they care more about the lives of First Nations people than they do a patch of worthy cloth. Sure, it's a protest but when did we give protesters the right to shock and confront us? The only person I gave that right to was Mr Stephen King.†

Perhaps we need to face that this was an act of violence—and perhaps even a hate crime—against a piece of blue fabric. This flag used to be a beloved symbol of freedom, not to mention a widely appreciated work of art.

The right-hand side is dominated by the Australian constellation, the Southern Cross. It's so uniquely Australian it's even used on the flags of New Zealand, Samoa, Papua New Guinea and Brazil, to show they were thinking about us at the time of design. This is without even including the German East Africa Company, which proudly waved the flag while attempting to dominate a large portion of modern Kenya—but this

---

*   I am not referring to the Budgie Nine's placement of a foreign flag on their taints. That's fine; if anything it's a great way to share our good old-fashioned larrikinism with the world.

†   I must admit, I did regret giving Stephen King contractual permission to jump out from behind corners and scare me whenever he desires but what's done is done. Perhaps someday I will read one of his books and see if they're just as scary.

was years before the Australian flag was even adopted, so the idea that it has a colonial history is absolute hogwash. The lower left of the flag features a star, awarded to us by King George V for our very good behaviour at the cessation of hostilities in World War I. And on the top left of our nation's flag is the most important feature of all: another nation's flag, the Union Jack, named after a young boy who first thought up the idea of Britain. Think of it as one of the first examples of sampling that later came to dominate modern hip-hop. Few nations would have the gall to just take another nation's flag and add it to their own but that's part of the Australian spirit. Nowadays they'd probably call it cultural appropriation but back then people would happily share each other's cultures. Heck, the British Empire spent the better part of a century enthusiastically sharing their culture with extreme prejudice.

Aesthetically, the Union Jack is an absolute delight. It has a shape and colour only matched by the fanciest brands of gel toothpaste. If you came across it on a foreign bottle, you would guess it indicated a strict instruction not to drink what was inside. However, when you know it symbolises the once-proud Empire, your heart trembles with what will probably turn out to be a devastating heart attack one of these days.

More than anything else, our flag represents Australia. It's time we were proud of Australia once again—and there is no better time to show this than on Australia Day. We should be raising our glorious flag proudly every Australia Day. Perhaps not the whole way, but at the very least to half mast. That's the level of respect this holiday deserves.

10 I'm Fairly Confident I've Worked Out the Gay Agenda

'Where does equality end? Tyranny!? If so, that's terrible.'

—PETER CHUDD, ADMIRABLY CONCERNED

Folktales tell us that at the end of every rainbow lies a pot of gold. However, I have seen the end of the rainbow agenda, and all that lies there is a civilisation in ruins.

Sure, from the distance the Rainbow Brigade seem harmless. Their very name could be taken from a Care Bears movie. But, just like Care Bears, when you get closer you discover that they're truly vicious animals ready to tear you limb from limb.

Of course, any criticism of this group is now labelled as 'hate speech'. Utterly laughable! I'm always incredibly polite when I'm arguing against a group's right to exist and self-determine. I speak decorously and keep my pinky raised.

The Rainbow Brigade like to claim that they're just looking for equality but once again I must ask: if everyone is equal, how will we know who is exceptional? Equality is an endorsement—we would be telling children that it is entirely okay for them to live openly however they please. These children would then grow up proud of who they are, without fear of reprisal. Their posture would crumble as they doubled over under the sheer weight of participation medals around their necks. The very thought chills me to my core.

We constantly hear that these groups are victims, but I'm almost certain that I'm the victim. The Rainbow Brigade can no longer say that they are unrepresented in this nation. They've now had consecutive prime ministers openly support their agenda. What more do they want? Results? Frankly, that's greedy.

Now we are seeing a unilateral assault by this dangerous group on one of the fundamental pillars of our modern lives: marriage. Marriage is the most important institution in our society, after the Department of Defence. It's one of our most important traditions and must be protected. You may argue all you wish but the simple fact of the matter is that marriage is defined as being between a man and a woman. This has been a cornerstone of civilised society and one of our longest traditions, dating all the way back to 2004, the year of *Shrek 2*.*

We can no longer deny that the Rainbow Agenda aims to bring down our society through the insidious tactic of attempting to have their love acknowledged by the state. Why must they demand marriage? Surely a civil union is just as reasonable an acknowledgement. It's separate but equal. It's like having your own water fountain, just for you. It shows you're a valued member of our society without the rest of us having to mix with you.

They claim to be on the side of love, yet the Rainbow Mafia have proven themselves to be utterly incapable of showing that love to me, a sweet and gentle patriot simply trying to live his own life in peace without being overrun by other people's attempts to do the same.

---

* Sadly, this film also features a deeply immoral relationship between a dragon and a donkey. Again, we see the effects of withering our marriage laws. Very amusing, though.

Instead, activist groups have repeatedly bombarded me with glitter, a substance security experts refer to as Gay Anthrax. Once you're struck by the shiny dust you are forever marked, doomed to sparkle in the sunshine until the day you die. It's not the first time these radicals attacked me. I had previously been attacked because I dared to criticise the tactics of the Rainbow Left through a harmless and accurate analogy, pointing out that they're exactly like Nazis, goose-stepping in rainbow uniforms. It's a perfectly apt comparison. Just like the Nazis, same-sex marriage stormtroopers are demanding to be acknowledged on a public stage, infiltrating our most sacred institutions and have invaded Denmark with an eye on Norway. Sadly—and predictably—there were petulant cries of outrage simply because the Nazis may have slightly specifically targeted homosexuals for extermination. But it's ridiculous to suggest I would endorse such a measure! I'd be satisfied with an internment camp. Unsurprisingly, the Rainbow Mafia would not listen, and instead attacked and attacked. Not unlike a certain German military force.[*]

They call me a hypocrite for claiming to endorse marriage as an important pillar of our society yet trying to deny others the right to enter the institution. This is the worst straw man I've seen outside Burning Man. Just because I support marriage doesn't mean I necessarily support all marriages. I'm in favour of *correct* marriages. *Proper* marriages. The kind of marriage that takes place at 3 a.m. in a Las Vegas drive-thru and is then annulled two days later. You know, marriage the way God intended it.

If we allow these lesser marriages we dilute the strength of our current marriages. The entire institution will lose its significance. It's just like I told my wife during our wedding vows some thirty-five years ago:[†]

---

[*]   I'm referring here to the Nazis in quite a clever and subtle way.

[†]   Or thirty-six or whatever. I can't really remember. What's important is it happened.

I, Peter Chudd, take you,
Soon-to-be Mrs Chudd,
To have and to hold,
From this day forward,
For better, for worse,
For rich, or richer,
In sickness and in health,
Until death do us part,
Unless one day
A same-sex couple
Makes the same vow
In which case, all bets are off.

This is why it's so upsetting when the Rainbow Left tries to claim that same-sex marriage does not affect me. Of course it does! The knowledge that Carl and Bruce from over the road have kicked down the door of my local parish and held the priest at knifepoint until he agreed to marry them affects me greatly, even if it hasn't happened yet. To know that they each have a ring around their finger makes the ring around my finger mean a little less. The club is less exclusive if we just let anyone in. It's a little like when you find a favourite lunch spot and have a few wonderful weeks in peace and quiet and then some lout in the restaurant review pages blows your secret and suddenly your little haven is filled with gays.* In fact, it's exactly like that.

It's our duty to ask where relaxing these laws will lead. Where will this end? With marriage? Sure, probably. But what if it doesn't? What's to be next, incest and bestiality? It does seem like a bit of a jump for that to be the very next thing but if it is then that's shocking. Imagine that: a couple in a long-term relationship asking to be married are

---

*   No, I still haven't forgiven you for this, Shannon.

secretly advocating marrying horses instead of each other. This is the sick hidden agenda of this movement.

It's shocking to me that the Rainbow Crusaders are incapable of seeing the logic of this argument, particularly given they've had so long to grapple with it. It's exactly the same argument I was using when I claimed that interracial marriage would lead to the death of society.

As much as the Left would love to remove religion from our society and place Jesus Christ in a choke-hold to force him to watch two men kissing, we cannot forget that I believe this is a Christian nation. Marriage is an institution created by God for the Christian church—or, at the very least, heavily plagiarised by God from other cultures. Still, this was long before intellectual property law so it's as good as Christian anyway.

Just because someone doesn't believe in our religion doesn't mean they shouldn't be held to its laws and values. This isn't a new thought. It's what I tell my waitress every Sunday morning when I insist that she should be stoned to death for daring to work the Sabbath.

This moral fortitude is what preserves our free society from those adhering to other religions* coming here and trying to make us all follow their laws! What nerve, to try to make someone not of their faith abide by their laws. It's one of the greatest moral crises of our time.

Yet we see the same bullying tactics being used by the Rainbow Brigade, the most horrendous of which is the completely true and definitely accurate claims of honest bakers being forced at gunpoint to make cakes for same-sex weddings. You would think that if the situation ever truly did arise where a baker was conscientiously objecting to someone's marriage on the basis of their sexuality, those participating in the wedding would take their money elsewhere. Instead, the Rainbow

---

* I mean Muslims but cannot say the word 'Muslim' lest I am arrested for being too truthful.

Brigade prefer to specifically seek out these bakeries because, in their own words, cake tastes better when it's made by a bigot.

But the strong-arming doesn't end there! Not satisfied with forcing their lifestyle down the throats of people trying to force cake down our throats, the Rainbow Brigade have also taken it upon themselves to start brainwashing children. The Safe Schools program may claim that it will save the lives of LGBTI+ youth, and that's all well and good, but it should require a parent's informed consent. We should be allowed to object to our children learning about these things. Sure, the children of parents who would object to an anti-bullying program would probably be the ones most needing education on the topic, but that's beside the point. We're talking about the rights of the parents, not the safety of children.

I do not send my children to school to have their minds filled with ideas. I do not require my child to be a free-thinking butterfly with grand ideas about civics and society. I require my human pets to be beaten into subservience. I created this creature and would like to have it trained as you would a dog. Were my beloved pooch Alexander to come back from his dog trainer confused about the constructs of gender in our society, I would be most disappointed.

That children could be taught things about their world without the express permission of their parents is disgusting. When it came to my own husky boy, Rand, I decided to take action. Now, his teacher knows to not dare move on to a new aspect of algebra without first checking with me.

Conservative MP George Christensen has already revealed that the Safe Schools program links to websites that are only a few clicks away from explicit material and I can confirm this is true. Just the other morning I settled in to uncover exactly what our children were being taught and discovered that if you visit the main page of a recommended Safe Schools website, with just a few clicks you can find yourself at the Google homepage. An adventurous student could then type 'hot vids of cock and ball torture' into the search bar and be bombarded with explicit material as shocking as it is arousing.

But perhaps the most upsetting part is that all this attention on LGBTI+ youth misses those really in need of special support: the conservative children who are trying to get an education and grow up to write bland letters to the *Adelaide Advertiser* without being exposed to other points of view. Where is the Safe Schools program for them? Think of the sweet children born into conservative families who just want to go to school until child labour laws are repealed and they can get a job. It breaks my heart to imagine these innocent progeny being pushed into the mud, their blazers ruined, their boater hats thrown into the lake, their pocket watches fed to a cow. To be conservative on the playground is to be a target. Nowadays, you can't stand on the back oval of your local school and loudly declare, 'I trust the neoclassical school of economic thought,' without being mercilessly bullied.

To this end, I have taken the liberty of drawing up a syllabus for a remade Safe Schools program to end the persecution of conservatives in our schools:

- *The demonisation of the conservative.* We will encourage students to reflect on their own behaviour and personalities and ask themselves if living their lives freely is somehow imposing on the more conservative members of their classroom. Students will practise being more subdued with their burgeoning self-discovery so as not to make a fuss.
- *How being wealthy can sometimes be harder than being poor.* This will introduce students to some of the trials and tribulations of having an abundance of wealth that would be unfamiliar to them. Students will understand the burden of expectation that comes with opportunity and the dreaded paradox of choice.
- *Acting normal.* Now we get to the heart of the course. Of course, as a staunch believer in personal freedom I would never ask anyone to

deny their true self. This course will help students to embrace their inner selves in a way that does not interfere with everyone else just trying to get on with being normal. Students will learn how to just keep to themselves and not bother anyone else with their desperate need for understanding and companionship.

- *Being less sensitive.* Nothing hurts my feelings more than the overly sensitive. This course aims to eradicate feelings that I do not believe to be worthwhile. For this section I will test the students personally. They will be given a basic labouring task to perform while I personally vilify them. Students wishing to pass the course will have to finish building their project without stopping to complain or wipe the tears from their eyes.

This is what is necessary to ensure the safety of the true victims in the playground. As long as a child can still legally be called names for using a bubbler to describe Reaganomics, I will fight. I will not rest until it is safe for an eight-year-old to wear a bowtie during physical education. I will not stop until I know that the only people being victimised on a playground are the ones whom I don't care about.

11 | Tomorrow Belongs to My Ideas

'Who are the real Nazis? The Nazis or the people who oppose the Nazis in a mean way?'

—PETER CHUDD, ERUDITELY

We live in uncertain times.

So said Werner Heisenberg, as he observed the rise of Adolf Hitler.[*] It's difficult for even me, a master of certainty, to accurately foretell what might happen next. I'd love to be able to say the answer will be what it always should have been—that people will start listening to me and the whole world will be fixed in a month or so—but there's a small chance that this won't happen.

Our political climate is becoming increasingly fractured, mostly due to the far Left refusing to join me on my journey further and further to the Right. We now have people resorting to reading Fake News instead of my much more worthwhile News Plus system, in which the facts are enhanced by my interpretation.

Mostly, it seems that people are scared. Usually, this is a great thing. Keeping people frightened can really help get some important legislation

---

[*] This scene is performed beautifully by Bryan Cranston and I highly recommend it.

passed. This time, however, it's slightly different. People seem to be concerned about the fresh rise of fascism around the world. I'll admit, it's a complicated situation for me, too. The German fascist party had the word 'socialist' in their name so I know to hate them by instinct, but here in Australia it's not so simple. I was at once angry that these neo-fascists had stolen my ideas and also flattered that someone had been reading my columns. As the months wore on I became frightened that plunging the world into another conflict might dramatically reduce my readership. Even my iron stomach turns a little at some of the positions expounded by these people but, equally, think of the merchandising opportunity. It's a very tough situation!

This is why I have decided that my form of resistance will be tacit endorsement. I understand that some people wish to oppose fascism instead of trying to use it to their advantage and I respect their opinion, though it is clearly a missed opportunity and therefore frankly wasteful.

Unfortunately, we've seen this opposition turn far too aggressive, such as on the very day of President Donald Trump's 2017 inauguration. The ABC happened to be broadcasting a live interview with one of the creators of the alt-right YungNazi movement. The interview was thoughtful and informative, providing real insight into which people needed to be rounded up into forced labour camps. However, it was brought to an abrupt halt when a member of the violent Left chose to punch the interviewee in the face.

This should never have been broadcast, even though I understand that, in the interest of balance, the ABC requires anyone expressing a fascist opinion to be immediately punched in the mouth.

Sure, I am as shocked as anyone to see the rise of fascism but we must ask ourselves, if one person is a Nazi but polite, and the other is liberal but violent, then who is the real threat to our future? Of course, the answer is still obviously the Nazis but it's worth pondering.

It's a real shame the formerly pious Left have turned violent. This form of resistance is completely undermining the whole movement! Were it up to me, I'd placidly accept the situation and just argue the point for as long as I'm allowed to speak before disappearing into a black site never to be seen again.

Still, as even these bleeding hearts look to me for guidance, I have a few notes for anyone wishing to stand in opposition to the rising tide:

1   *Be civil.* I cannot stress this enough. You cannot be mean to the Nazis. They're famously delicate and need to be addressed politely at all times. Be sure to treat them with the utmost respect and *listen* to exactly why they believe your people should be wiped from the face of the Earth before you make any snap judgements.

2   *Do not resort to violence.* The supposedly tolerant Left have started to take joy in responding to Nazis with physical violence. How uncivilised. Previous generations would have never responded to the threat of fascism with violence! They would have stormed the beaches of Normandy and then insisted on a robust exchange of ideas. You'll hear people argue that engaging in rational debate legitimises fascism and leave you helpless to counter it, as has been exploited before, but we really do owe it to ourselves to try one more time. We have to consider the fact that some people are Nazis because they haven't heard in their decades of life that racism is wrong. If we simply educate them everything will be fine. Remember, if you use violence to repel Nazis you are exactly as bad as the Nazis. Instead, hold strong to your good ideas as the storm troopers march up your driveway.

3   *Only protest respectfully.* Yes, human life has a great worth but so do windows. Which of these is more important? Truthfully, I don't know, but I will say that it's free to make new people. The fact of the matter is that if anyone in your protest numbering tens of thousands of people causes any kind of damage to public property the entire protest is instantly illegitimate. It's part of the insurance

contract of any protest. Battles for civil rights, equal opportunity and against tyranny of all kinds have been lost purely because someone threw a brick. The only reason to take to the streets and destroy public property is if your sports team wins something. That's a jovial expression of pure happiness that lifts everyone's spirits. Windows broken in triumph are easily defensible, but windows broken in anger? That's terrible.

4 *Don't give them any ideas.* This is why violence is such a problem. If the opponents of fascism resort to punching you're going to make the Nazis realise that punching is an option. Before these protestors brought violence into the equation no one had any idea it even existed! It was a pure Cain and Abel situation. Now, I'm worried that their stated aim to purge other human beings might end up being violent in some way.

5 *Just act as if everything is fine.* This tactic is most useful if you, like me, don't really have a dog in the fight. I'm lucky enough to be completely untouched by this whole situation and can just sit it out if it gets too hard for me. Sure, everyone else will claim it's my duty as a human being to get in the fight but that seems really difficult and will force me to make some uncomfortable choices. What I'm saying is, I'm just going to put myself first and do what I want to do without any concern for other people. But, importantly, if I see other people actually trying to make a difference in any way I don't personally approve of, I'm going to condemn them. That's my role for now. I'm going to be the civility police for the side opposing the Nazis. I'm sure this will be remembered fondly one day.

The truth of the matter is no one can know for sure what tomorrow brings. We will all need to safeguard ourselves for the future. Luckily, my opinions have held for sixty years now and promise to be just as relevant tomorrow as they are today. With those by my side and a fully stocked bomb shelter in my basement* I'm certain I will be okay.

In this book I've attempted to impart to you my knowledge and wisdom to help you survive and prosper in the modern world but even I cannot say for sure if this will be enough to prepare you for what's on the horizon. That's why it's so important for you to buy extra copies of this book, my DVD special, and also my merchandise. Now is not the time to look away. It's the time to get on the phone and harass my publishers about another book deal so that I can continue to keep you abreast of what you should think.

I'd like to sincerely thank you for purchasing this book, as well as any additional copies of this book. Without my dear audience I would simply be ordinary scum like the rest of you. It's your devotion that keeps my voice alive, despite years of screaming which have worn my vocal cords down to a growl akin to a flooded lawnmower or a late Bob Dylan album.

I can promise you this: my voice will not disappear. I will not be silenced. For as long as there is air in my lungs I will be forcing that air out through my collapsed throat and inspiring the good people of this country the only way I know how: through the high-pitched warble of an oppressed white male.

---

* Remember, dear readers, in the most dire of circumstances, if it really comes down to it, you are not welcome in my shelter. If you wish to help, though, please inform me of the location of yours and what resources you have that can be plundered.

Peter Chudd is the most important and underappreciated thinker in the country. He's most notable as the only true voice of reason left in Australia. This is the first book Peter has been able to publish without the political correctness police burning it for being dangerously insightful.

James Colley is a Young Walkley-nominated satirist and creator of both SBS Comedy's *The Backburner* and Nailed It! at Giant Dwarf. He works on ABC TV's *The Weekly with Charlie Pickering* and *Gruen*, and has performed at the Festival of Dangerous Ideas, the St. James Ethics Centre and Splendour in the Grass, among others. He has also had multiple sold-out seasons at the Sydney Comedy Festival.